CHRIST'S APPEAL
FOR LOVE

CHRIST'S APPEAL FOR LOVE

To His Humble Servant Josefa Menéndez

Religious of the Sacred Heart

Translated by L. Keppel

Albatross Publishers
Naples, Italy
2020

Originally Published in London by
Sands & CO., 1942

ISBN 978-1-946963-41-3

Letter from the Cardinal Protector
H.E. CARDINAL E. PACELLI
(*Now H. H. Pope Pius XII happily reigning*)
April, 1938

To the Reverend Mother Superior General S.S.H.

VERY REVEREND MOTHER,

I have no doubt whatever that the publication of these pages, filled as they are with the great love which His grace inspired in His very humble servant MARIA JOSEFA MENÉNDEZ, will be agreeable to His SACRED HEART:

May they efficaciously contribute to develop in many souls a confidence ever more complete and loving in the infinite mercy of this Divine Heart towards the poor sinners that we all are.

Such are the good wishes which, with my blessing, I send you and all the Society of the SACRED HEART.

E. CARD. PACELLI.

INTRODUCTION

THE appeal of LOVE and MERCY transmitted to the world in the following pages was confided by Our Blessed Lord to a little Sister of the Sacred Heart, Josefa Menéndez, who died at Poitiers aged thirty-three years, on the 29th of December 1923.

Up to the present time they have remained unknown, treasured by the Society to which she belonged. The many favours due to the intercession of this humble Sister have given them increased authority, and with the permission of the Church they are now published.

God willed to hide from all eyes, and for many years, His chosen instrument: "What art thou," He was wont to say to her, "but an echo of My Voice . . . ? and when My Voice is no longer heard . . . what of thee?"

If to-day the veil which hid her is raised, it is less in the hope of making her known than of revealing to the world the desire of the Sacred Heart of JESUS that all should be attracted and saved by the ever-renewed efforts of a consuming and merciful Love.

PART I

BIOGRAPHICAL SKETCH OF THE LIFE OF SISTER JOSEFA MENÉNDEZ, R.S.C.J.

CHAPTER I

On February 4th, 1890, a child was born in Madrid who was destined in God's Providence to be the loved and privileged confidante of the Sacred Heart of Our Lord.

Josefa Menéndez was of humble parentage, but thanks to the intelligence and energy of the head of the family, she knew no want, and her first years were passed in a carefree and happy atmosphere of faith and honest labour, to both of which she was early trained. She was only five when she was confirmed, and at seven she made her first confession. In later years she used ingenuously to recall the date of that event, a First Friday in October, 1897, exclaiming regretfully: "If only I could feel such contrition for my sins as I had on that day!" The little girl's confessor, Father Rubio, who later joined the Company of Jesus, was struck by the spirituality of his little penitent, and he carefully cultivated her aptitude for prayer and taught her how to meditate on Our Lord's life and sufferings, and in this she made great progress.

Josefa, however, was not of the goody-goody type, and her spirited and playful assumption of authority over her three little sisters asserted itself freely, and the often harassed mother would proudly trust her eldest to replace her, while her father, whose special pet she was, dubbed her his "Little Empress," refusing her nothing, a fact well known and exploited by the younger ones, who always had recourse to her intercession when some favour was hoped for. So precocious was the child's intelligence that her parents fondly hoped to have her trained for the teaching profession. This, however, was not to be, as we shall see—Our Lord had His own divine and very special designs for her future.

When Josefa was eleven years of age, began the all-important preparation for First Communion. The very thought of it was an enthralling delight to the spiritual-minded and thoughtful child, who now began to attend the instructions given at the Réparatrice Convent. The great day was preceded by a short retreat, and we still possess the "notes" on what she afterwards termed "The first appeal" made to her by the Lover of her soul.

"In my first meditation I reflected on the words 'Jesus wants to give Himself to me, that I may be wholly His.' What joy, I thought, He is the one object of my desires—yet how is it to be done? I consulted one of the Mothers, and she explained to me that I must be very, very good, and that thus I should always belong entirely to Our Lord.

"The subject of meditation on the second day was 'Jesus, Spouse of Virgins, takes delight in the pure and innocent.' This was a great light to me—the solution of yesterday's puzzle; of course I must become His little Spouse, then indeed I would belong entirely to Him, just as Mummy belonged to Daddy—so I there and then promised Our Lord ever to remain a virgin (I did not understand what it meant) that I might ever be entirely His. All day long I renewed this promise, and in the evening made a consecration of myself to the Child JESUS during Benediction, asking with great

fervour that I might be wholly and entirely His. That
I was soon to receive Him in my heart by Holy Communion filled me with a strange ecstasy, and while I
was silently revelling in the happy thought I heard a
voice that I can never forget saying to me: 'Yea, little
one, I want thee to be all Mine.' What then happened
it is impossible for me to put into words, but when I
left the chapel my mind was quite made up—I would
be *very*, *very* good!

"Of vocation I had never heard, and I thought
nuns were unearthly beings quite apart, but from that
time onward something seemed to set me, too, apart,
and this feeling remained. It was only long afterwards
that I knew it had been a vocation to religious life.

"On the third day of the retreat I renewed my resolution, and on St. Joseph's day, the happy day of my
First Communion, I made this offering—and it came
from my very inmost being:

" 'On this day, March 19th, 1901, before all heaven
and earth, I take as my witness my heavenly Mother
Mary, and St. Joseph, my Advocate and Father, I promise Jesus that I will ever safeguard in me the precious
virtue of virginity, my only desire being to please
Him, and my only fear that of offending Him by sin.
Show me, O my God, how to belong wholly to You in
the most perfect manner possible, that I may ever love
You more and more and never displease You in anything. This is the desire of my heart, on this my First
Communion day. Holy Mary, obtain its fulfilment on
the Feast of your holy Spouse, St. Joseph.' I duly
wrote and signed it, and at every subsequent Communion I renewed this offering. When, afterwards, I

told Father Rubio what I had done, he explained to me that little girls should not make promises beyond that of being very good, and he wanted me to tear up the paper. I could not, and I continued to repeat: 'Lord, I am yours for ever'."

This witness of her first oblation was kept by Josefa till her dying day, and the little faded paper, covered with her large childish script, still bears witness to her faithful love.

At about this time her parents apprenticed her to a School of Arts and Crafts "Fomente del Arte," where her intelligence and readiness in learning soon attracted attention. Her clever fingers turned out marvels of needlecraft, and success crowned her efforts; still her heart remained unsullied, and she obtained the strength she needed for the fight in her daily Communion. "I went through many perils," she once said, "but God always protected me amid the dangers of evil talk, so common in our workroom. It often made my tears flow to hear things which troubled me discussed, but I never doubted that God meant me to be His Own, and it was my comfort and strength. Nothing and nobody could have altered my resolve or made me doubt its truth.

When Josefa was fifteen she was already an accomplished needlewoman and her parents took her home. They were now living near the School of the Sacred Heart (Leganitos), where the younger ones were being taught. The Convent chapel drew her powerfully, and daily she visited it. The hidden Presence in the Tabernacle was beginning to attract her in a definite direction, that of His Sacred Heart.

The happiness of her home had hitherto been unimpaired. Josefa spent her laborious days in needlework and in helping her mother. Her father's predilection for his little "Empress" made the home ties sweet and strong, and she grew daily in affection both for her parents and little sisters. She was so gay and full of spirits, so unselfish and thoughtful, that she was the very soul of the little family, where Faith and contentment continued to reign supreme.

The great treat of those days was a visit to the Carmel of Loeches, where the children had an aunt. They were received like little princesses and had the run of the Chaplain's quarters, where they discovered a copy of the Carmelite Rule, which they eagerly read. On their return home the prime game was to play at being Carmelites. Office was chanted, penances performed, in all of which Josefa was the leading spirit—but it was for her a good deal more than a mere game.

But suffering was needed to forge the instrument God had chosen for Himself—the winds of tribulation began to blow, testing the budding fruit. "Never doubt the love of My Heart," Our Lord was to say to her later. "What matter if the winds blow and buffet thee: I Myself have rooted thy littleness in the soil of My Heart."

CHAPTER II

SUFFERING now came on Josefa in the form of family reverses. Under its pressure her character gained in firmness, her self-control increased, and her love grew stronger from its contact with the Cross.

In 1907 one of her younger sisters, Carmen, aged only twelve, died. The first blow was followed within a few weeks by another, the death of the children's grandmother. Carmencita's loss was like a death-knell to her parents; both father and mother were laid low, the one by typhoid fever, the other by congestion of the lungs. Josefa's true worth was at once revealed; she gave up her work and divided her attention between the two invalids, the care of her sisters and the manifold home duties that pressed on her young shoulders. Medical advice was costly, and soon ran away with all their savings. Poverty was now added to sickness, yet not for a moment did Josefa's courage flinch, and for a period of well-nigh seven weeks she bore unaided the full responsibility of anxiety and privation.

"We all slept together on a mattress on the floor," she said; "our kind doctor wanted Father and Mother to be taken to hospital, but I did not consent, for I was certain Providence would not forsake us, and It came to our help through the nuns of the Sacred Heart. Oh! I shall never forget how good they were to us." A novena to St. Madeleine Sophie Barat was begun,

18

and in the course of it the mother, whose life was now despaired of, called the family to her bedside. "Do not cry," she said: "Mother Barat has just been here to visit me—she told me that I am not going to die, because you still need my presence." "We never heard the particulars," Josefa said afterwards, "but the next day she was out of danger, and Father got well too, but his strength was gone and he never was able to work again."

On Josefa fell henceforward the full burden of supporting the whole family; comfort and easy circumstances were things of the past. The nuns gave her a sewing machine and obtained work for her. She already had a reputation for clever dressmaking, and before long had more orders than she could attend to, which spelled for her days of uninterrupted labour, prolonged far into the night; her energy and self-denial were equal to the occasion, and her earnings gradually brought a measure of alleviation to their poverty. The respite was of short duration; her father was carried off by a heart attack and died a holy death, assisted by Father Rubio, who from that time onward remained both counsellor and friend of the family. More than ever Josefa became the sole comfort of her mother.

Misfortune in no way quenched Josefa's ardour for the things of the spirit; daily she repeated the offering she had made of herself as a child of eleven, and it gave her strength to forge on towards the goal of her desires. Even before her father's death she had begged to be allowed to follow her vocation to the "Sacred Heart," but the request had made her father angry for the first time in his life with "Pepa," and yet he was a good Catholic! but not prepared to give up his child of predilection; so Josefa dried her tears and for the moment spoke no more of her secret aspirations.

Later on a Carmelite Father offered to obtain her admission among the Carmelites; but she knew she was not called to be a daughter of St. Teresa, so she gratefully declined, but seized the opportunity to state once more to her mother where her true vocation lay. The poor woman tearfully begged her not to abandon her. Josefa allowed herself to be persuaded, and once more consented to postpone her departure. Great was her deception, however, when her younger sister obtained the coveted leave, and left home for the noviceship of Chamartin (Madrid). She had specially trained this sister with a view to her taking her place, and it was a terrible blow to her. Only the selflessness of her love of God helped her to bear up under the keen disappointment she experienced.

The old life was resumed; this time with the help of her last remaining sister; orders so abounded that it took her all her strength and the whole of her time to carry them out. The Divine Will was leading her by hidden paths, slowly but surely, and yet another frustration of her hopes came to her.

Father Rubio, who had followed her up for the last twelve years, had never ceased to take an interest in her. In 1912 he judged the moment opportune: the Order of Marie Réparatrice seemed to him one that would suit Josefa; he knew the nuns intimately, and began to direct her vocation towards them. Josefa was twenty-two, and though her attraction lay in a different direction, she stifled her feelings and asked to be admitted at the Réparatrice Convent. The spirit and practice satisfied her aspirations, and she generously embraced her new religious life. The thought of making reparation for the sins of men through the Heart of Mary appealed to her, and no sort of temptation or trouble came to mar the happy months that followed. Gradually, however, and almost in spite of herself, there stole over her soul's consciousness the reawakening of another love—that of the Sacred Heart—her first attraction, and every time she heard the Convent bells ringing (for they were close to her Convent) the inward struggle was renewed. Our Lady herself intervened.

Josefa was in charge of a large room which contained a big statue of Our Lady of Sorrows; in accordance with Spanish custom, it was adorned with rich vesture, and in her hand Our Lady held a crown of natural thorns. Josefa was surprised one day to see the crown lit up by a shaft of light coming from she knew not where. At first she did not venture to speak of the marvel, but as it continued she decided to investigate the origin of the light. She found that it proceeded from one of the thorns, and at the same time she heard a penetrating voice saying: "Take this thorn, my child; Jesus will give you others as time goes on."

Josefa detached the thorn as she was bid, and the response she gave to her Mother's gift was a fresh offering of herself, which was before long to receive its seal in suffering.

Her six months' postulantship was over and the day of her clothing fixed, when her mother, who had sorely missed her, came and claimed her back. Father Rubio seconded the mother's request, and so it came about that Josefa's return home was decided, and she left the noviciate with the feelings we can imagine. She took with her the thorn, whose light, like that in her own heart, was quenched. Deeply the reality had sunk into her inmost being—and this reality was suffering.

Courageously she faced the upward path to God, and resumed the old tasks. This time she was employed very largely by the nuns of the Sacred Heart in making the children's uniforms. Simple, modest and conscientious in her work, her life was illumined by her constant prayer. The nun who was over her in the School linen-room was struck by her devotedness, her love of duty and the sweetness of disposition that made light of every difficulty and never caused the smallest embarrassment to others. Her tact, her dexterity and judgment, her silent activity greatly impressed her; she was always on the watch to render service, and every spare minute was spent before the Blessed Sacrament. "I feel thoroughly in my element when I am here," she used to say in speaking of Chamartin. Very different was the story when obliged to work for clients outside. Her delicate conscience was many a time outraged by the absence of modesty in dress of those she worked for, and who as Catholics should have known better; it was then that she more than at any other time felt her "banishment" from Convent walls, and she would exclaim: "Since childhood my one prayer has been 'that I might dwell in the House of the Lord,' and the more I see of life outside, the greater is my longing to die if this wish of my heart cannot be granted."

She lived on her burning hopes, and her daily Communion was fuel to the fire; there lay the secret of her serenity and of her strength; to others, the secret of her cross and of her thorn was never told.

Josefa was not one to make many friends, but by her example and counsel she had become the centre of a group of working-girls on whom her influence was remarkable. She would head a pilgrimage to Avila or to the Cerre de los Angeles, where the memorial to the Sacred Heart had been erected in accomplishment of the National Vow, and in these and other rare outings her bright cheerfulness and fervour made a deep impression for good on them.

The months dragged on, and all the time Josefa was watching her opportunity. In 1917 she thought the moment had come, and when she begged her admission at Chamartin she was kindly received and her mother's consent obtained. Her departure was fixed for the 24th of September, Feast of Our Lady of Mercy. Alas! when the long desired day dawned her mother's tears shook her resolution, and again prevailed . . . , tender-hearted Josefa yielded at the sight of her distress; her place in the noviceship remained empty, and she was left to weep over the frailty that had prevented her from keeping the tryst. But the Divine Lover of her soul pursued His purpose in her regard and in His own good time was to bring her out of darkness into light.

The French houses of the Sacred Heart which had been suppressed were just at this time taking on a new lease of life, and many were reopening after the expulsions that had marked the beginning of the century. The old monastery of the Feuillants at Poitiers had been preserved to the Society, and it was here that a novice-ship for coadjutrix Sisters was to open, in the house that had been the first noviceship of the Sacred Heart and was still redolent with memories of St. Madeleine Sophie. Josefa felt that if ever she was to regain admit-tance to religious life she must lose no more time, so she applied once more at Chamartin for admission, but she was refused. It was in 1919, and she was already twenty-nine years of age. She feared this result, and felt she had forfeited her chance of success by her former act. What was she to do? An interior voice urged her to try and try again, but an irrevocable denial met her advances; Superiors mistrusted her long and repeated hesitations. She tells us herself what happened: "On the 16th of September I felt my courage at an end, and kneeling before my crucifix, I begged Our Lord either to take me out of this life or admit me into the Society of His Sacred Heart, for I could bear no more.

"Then it seemed to me that He showed me His Sacred Hands and Feet, and said to me: 'Kiss these Wounds. Canst thou indeed bear no more for Me? Have I not chosen thee for My Sacred Heart?'

"I am unable to put into words what then took place in me. I promised—Oh! I promised Him to live hence-forth only for Him and to suffer . . . and begged Him to pity my weakness and wavering."

Two months passed in fervent supplications till there dawned a memorable day for Josefa; it was the 19th of November, and in her Communion that morn-ing she again implored Our Lord by His Wounds and

Precious Blood to open the doors of the Sacred Heart to her, which she knew she had closed by her own act.

That morning Josefa went as usual to fetch work at the Convent at Chamartin; on her arrival she was told that the Superior wished to see her: a letter had just arrived from Poitiers (Les Feuillants, spoken of above), asking for one or two good vocations to start the projected noviceship—did they know of any, and could they send anyone? The Superior asked her if she felt equal to entering in a French house of the Society. This time there was no hesitation; at once she wrote to offer herself, and kneeling before the Blessed Sacrament, she begged that grace and strength should be given her to triumph over her weakness. This prayer was answered, and she was able to say afterwards: "I felt endued with a strength I had never before experienced."

Her broken-hearted mother this time offered no opposition; and in order to avoid painful scenes, Josefa left home carrying nothing with her and without saying good-bye.

The Mothers at Chamartin gave her her fare and provided her with all she needed—she reached San Sebastian, the first stage of her journey, and there found a warm welcome in the Sacred Heart. Her stay in that house was prolonged for a whole month, probably waiting for a fellow traveller, as she knew no French. She was deeply grateful to have at last reached the haven of her desires, and devoted herself to helping in the household. The nuns noted how silently and deftly she worked, always in deep recollection. Letters from home left her unmoved, though she was far from being insensible to them. Her ignorance of French alone worried her a little, but God's guidance was too palpable to allow her inward peace to be disturbed, and on February the 4th, 1920, she left for France. It was a final departure, for she never saw Spain again. But what of that? Was she not obeying the call of One whose sovereign love can never ask too much?

CHAPTER III

THE old-world town of Poitiers is perched above the valley of the Clain, and from the top of its highest hill the ancient monastery of the Feuillants dominates the surrounding country. There, two centuries earlier, a colony of Cistercians had settled; it was a place of prayer and labour, but the French Revolution left the hallowed spot desolate. It was, however, destined to live again, and when the storm had passed and faith had revived, the monastic buildings were peopled once more at the coming of St. Madeleine Sophie and her newly-founded Order. Here the Saint opened the first noviceship of the Society of the Sacred Heart, here she made long sojourns, and it was to be the scene of many graces conferred on her. Ever since it has been regarded by the nuns of the Sacred Heart as a sort of reliquary and memorial of their holy Foundress. To this remote and solitary house of prayer Josefa was guided by God, that He might there cultivate her soul and train and associate her with His divine Heart in the work of Redemption.

None of those who saw Josefa on her arrival at Poitiers could have suspected how great a work was beginning, for from the very first days of her postulant-ship she passed unnoticed, and during the four years of her short religious life remained ever the same simple, silent, laborious and unassuming religious. There was nothing particularly attractive in her

27

exterior, and she seemed at times to be suffering, but a bright, intelligent smile broadened on her face when addressed, especially if a service were asked of her, and relieved the seriousness which was the usual expression of her countenance. Her large dark eyes alone expressed and at times betrayed her inmost feelings; they were limpid eyes, gentle and ardent, and bespoke her interior recollection. Her gifts, if hidden, were very real ones: she was swift and adroit, active and adaptable to all sorts of conditions; she possessed rare good sense and excellent judgment. These gave her character an earnest and balanced foundation on which grace could build at will. Her heart was both tender and generous; her past sufferings had given her breadth and understanding and that kindliness which self-forgetfulness alone engenders. She brought to her religious formation a maturity which was the fruit of sacrifice, a supernatural understanding of the value of religious vocation, together with a highly-developed interior spirit and an immense love of God.

These gifts were as hidden from herself as they were from those around her, and from the day of her arrival till that of her death she passed utterly unknown on her way, in the complete effacement of a very faithful and obscure life.

There were few novices at Poitiers; Josefa remained first postulant and eldest novice among the members culled like herself from various houses of the Society.

The humble hiddenness of the life filled her with enthusiasm; it was modelled on that of Nazareth, and she found in it the fulfilment of her most sanguine expectations; it was, in effect, just what St. Madeleine

Sophie had defined as her ideal—a great deal of strenuous labour offered for the souls of children, accompanied by the vivifying charity and prayerful atmosphere that result from close union with the Heart of Jesus.

Events were few, and there is little to record of the months of her postulantship and noviceship, and the short eighteen months of religious life that followed after her vows till her death. None of the things that made up her daily life are of any value in the eyes of the world, yet are not the first years of the life of the Man-God all summed up in one short sentence: "He was subject to them"? And so it was with Josefa; the less a Sister is spoken of, the truer she is to type; to be unknown, to be thought little of—is, after all, the highest praise that can be meted out to a Coadjutrix Sister of the Sacred Heart. None of those who lived with her knew anything of her mysterious intercourse with the Sacred Heart of Our Lord, and when after her death they were asked to recount all they could recall about her, how little they were able to say. She had passed unnoticed and hidden, simply and faithfully doing her duty—that was all.

She was employed in the kitchen, linen-room, at ironing and other household work, and the testimony of each was that she was perfect in the accomplishment of every duty—silent, docile, and distinguished in nothing but her fidelity. Yet her self-effacement in no way dulled her initiative and her marked aptitude for every kind of employment. This enabled her to get through a very large amount of work, and a great deal fell to her share—there was a finish and a deftness in all she undertook that left her leisure to help others, and she was always to the fore in emergencies when work of any kind called for special devotedness. She was the last to leave, too, and one could be sure that what she undertook would be well done and carried to a successful finish, especially if the work was tiring and arduous. An example will suffice. One day that there was a great press of work a Sister begged her to help her in a long piece of mending; regretfully she had to refuse, but with a tremendous effort she contrived to complete her own duties and gaily arrived in time to undertake over and above the service demanded of her. Thus she was always full of those thoughtful attentions that go so far in making charity perfect.

By nature she was gay and exuberant, so that it was a real suffering to her to be debarred at recreation from intercourse with others by her ignorance of French; but as soon as she became more or less familiar with it she amused them all by her quaint remarks, with never a trace of self-consciousness or human respect. She always gave a joyous turn to recreations, but tempered with exquisite tact and good sense, and in all things her insight into spiritual things was manifest.

Outside recreation hours, when gaiety is not only allowed, but a duty, she was remarked for a certain grave simplicity, and seemed as it were enveloped in the thought of God. Her whole attitude at prayer was impressive; the presence of Our Lord in the Blessed Sacrament was the irresistible magnet of her faith; and as she knelt with clasped hands and downcast eyes, entirely oblivious of all that went on around her, she unconsciously taught a lesson of deep recollection.

She was entrusted with the care of the little oratory that had once been the cell of St. Madeleine Sophie Barat, and also of a little chapel where the Blessed Sacrament was reserved; great was the loving care she lavished on their upkeep, and she was often heard to ejaculate in verses of the Psalms that expressed her fervent feelings, when she believed herself alone and unobserved. So well known was her thoroughness and the perfection she put into all her work, that she was often entrusted with things that required extra care and judgment, and at once they became to her of supreme interest. An old Mother who was hardly able to do anything for herself was entrusted to her solicitude, and for a long time she ministered to her wants, morning and evening attending to her and watching over her every need; she might have been her own mother, so respectful was the tenderness with which she surrounded her, striving to make her forget the length and severity of her trial.

It was not long before her services were enlisted in making the children's uniforms; so useful did she become in this respect, that gradually a small workroom was organised and conducted by her, and she was entrusted with the training of several of the novices after she had made her vows. Her patience was unwearied, and she was ever ready to repair mistakes and begin faulty work anew. She was glad of this opportunity of service to the Society, by which the novices became such useful members, and she strove to inculcate in them her own love of finished work. "We never saw her impatient or out of temper," was the testimony of one of them. "If work had been carelessly done, she would gently say: 'Don't let us ever do anything carelessly in Our Lord's service.' Her firm and gentle ways endeared her to us singularly, and we respected and loved her for the wonderful example she was to us all; the workroom was like a little oratory, and we were all busily employed and happy."

Josefa had a great love for children, and especially the smallest; it showed itself when she tried on their frocks. The children felt her affection and joy in serving them and appreciated her devotedness. How often she went through the dormitories at night to make sure that they had all that they required; she would stop a moment to sew on a button here, to mend a rent there, or to tidy up for some tired pickle too sleepy to do it for herself. All was done so quietly, so naturally, that it was taken as a matter of course, and contact with her humble devotedness had a happy influence on the children.

Busy as Josefa was all day, no sooner did she get a leisure moment than she straightway fell naturally to her prayers. One of the nuns came to her one night to ask a small service of her; she was sewing at the time, but her whole attitude betrayed the trend of her thoughts; she seemed lost in God. The mother stopped a few minutes, watching her, then gently called her. Sister Josefa started and came back with effort; her far away look told of her intimate converse with God; but rising swiftly, she listened to the message with the deference which was habitual to her, and at once set about doing what was required.

And so the days and months slipped by, and no

event of importance came to break the uniformity of her life. On the 16th of July, 1920, she received the habit, and thanks to the charity of the Mothers, both her mother and sister were able to be present at the ceremony. It was deep contentment to her affectionate heart, and she tried to make them share in the happiness she was experiencing. They came again when two years later she took her First Vows on the same day in 1922. They little suspected all that had passed between the humble religious and the Heart of Our Lord; it was her secret, and shrouded from every eye, except those of her Superiors.

Josefa returned once more to her hidden life, from which she was to emerge on two solitary occasions only. In May, 1923, it was decided to send her for a time to the house of noviceship at Marmoutiers. The month spent there sufficed to impress on the Mother in charge of the Sisters the depth and reality of her virtue. She wrote: "Sister Menéndez has won the esteem and affection of all the Sisters by her fidelity and by the cordiality of her intercourse with them. One cannot but guess how intimate is her union with Our Lord."

Sister Josefa was at home at once, and wherever there was work to be done or devotedness called for, there she was sure to be found.

Our Lord had said to her: "I will leave traces of thy passage in that house"—and it came about that circumstances occurred that brought into clear relief her deep religious spirit, and she left an impression of rare and exceptional virtue.

Physical disabilities from which Sister Josefa had

c—c

long suffered were much aggravated from that time on. Our Lord had warned her that her illness was incurable, and she already knew the secret of her approaching end, yet no word or sign betrayed this knowledge to those with whom she lived. Some, however, began to suspect that her condition was more grave than had been thought at first, for at times her face showed signs of utter exhaustion, and that in spite of the effort she made to conceal her sufferings.

She returned to the Feuillants only to start on another temporary absence. It was on the occasion of a Superiors' Retreat at the Mother House in Rome, and Sister Josefa was taken by hers to help, as all thought, with the extra housework such a gathering entailed; there was, however, another reason in the designs of God. Had He not said to her: "I direct all things, and I know that which will help on My work"? and later: "When, after a dull day, the sun once more shines forth, it appears to have increased its radiance, so after intense suffering that which I do will stand out with greater clearness." And so it came to pass, for in the enveloping silence Sister Josefa passed through hours of stress in Rome, succeeded by peace and light; surely the reward of unswerving faith in obedience, and in the blessing received from the Holy Father.

On the 26th of October she returned to Poitiers for the last short lap of her life's journey. She knew that it was so.

Once more the old avocations were resumed, and she worked on till her strength failed, hinting that the workroom she so loved was soon to see her no more.

On the 9th of December her hunger for Holy Communion gave her strength to drag herself to the chapel, but it was for the last time; that night she took to her bed for good.

She made her religious Profession at the same time as she was anointed for the last passage. Nothing marred her peace and happiness. "The veil began to be lifted, and she who was thought so little of, was shown in that hour to be a child of benediction," said one who was present. "Her room in the infirmary was a veritable little oratory, and the humble Sister, as one transfigured, in her agony. Though none could explain, we all felt that something wonderful was being enacted under our very eyes."

One of the Mothers wrote afterwards: "I saw her many times in the days that followed, and asked her one day to pray for the children's Retreat." "I love them so much," she said; "I like to hear them at their games, but more especially when I see them at Holy Communion, and know that Our Lord is in each of their hearts. Oh, yes, I shall indeed pray for them when I get to Heaven. . . . God has given me," she continued, as if to herself, "a heart that loves very much. . . . I love the Society and all the Mothers and Sisters . . . and the children; I *do* love them so;" all this was said with an accent of unmistakable sincerity and warm charity.

Another day she said: "The novices must be very, very fervent and energetic in their vocation. I myself had to fight so hard, and sometimes I felt as if I could not go on. When this happened I used to go to the Mother Assistant, after which I felt strengthened.

It cost me a lot to leave Spain, but what was that in comparison with my vocation—yes, I did it with all my heart. What we have to learn above all else in the noviceship is obedience—obedience in a spirit of faith," and she repeated this several times, as if scrutinising the motives in her own soul of that safe and sure way of obedience.

On another occasion, when she seemed to be in great pain, she said: "Our Lord wants us to endure in many ways . . . " and she continued: "I have suffered much, . . . " and here her voice took on a firmness that was quite unforgettable. "But one forgets it, one forgets the suffering . . . and now Our Lord is about to"—for a moment she stopped as if ashamed of what she had almost expressed—"Oh, no, not *reward* me . . . for what have I done to merit it? Nothing, absolutely nothing. . . . He is going to make me happy for ever." Her voice here died away into silence in the contemplation of such bliss. Then: "How good God is. Oh, how good!" And there was deep contentment in the expression of her love.

She wrote a last letter to her mother. In it she said: "I am glad to die, because I know it is His will. Then, too, because I long to see His face unveiled, and that is impossible here below. Do not be sad on my account, for death is the beginning of life, if we love and expect His coming. We shall not be parted for very long, for life is so short and we shall be together for all eternity. These four years of religious life have been just Heaven to me, and I would love the same happiness for my sisters, and know that it lies in doing God's Will. You must not think, either, that I am dying in pain and distress, for death seems to me . . . well, just love; nor do I feel ill, but I cannot live without Our Lord and our Blessed Lady."

To her sister who was, like herself, a nun of the Sacred Heart, she wrote more intimately: "I am happy, especially in the knowledge that I have done God's Will; it is true that He has led me through paths that were none of my choosing, but now at the end there is only joy and *such* peace!" She goes on to give some sisterly advice, and ends up by saying: "Do not let your wretchedness distress you; Our Lord is so good and loves us as we are. I have experienced it—have perfect trust in His goodness, love and mercy. The Society has indeed been a true and tender Mother to me. I have been treated with such wonderful consideration and kindness which I cannot repay here; but I shall obtain all I want for them from Our Lady when I get to Heaven. I love France; I have been very happy in this country; it has been the home of my soul, and in it I have received innumerable graces. We have always loved each other very much, dear Sister; we must part for a while. One day we shall be united again, and our bonds will be the stronger, for being not only sisters, but fellow-religious. Adieu."

Mysterious sufferings, a trial, a purgation that set the crown on her life, saw Sister Josefa's brief career come to an end. She died a few days later, alone and solitary. Our Lord had said to her: "Thou shalt suffer, and in deepest dereliction thou shalt die; seek for no alleviation, for it is I Myself that cause it." Thus ended the sacrifice of her faithful love—it was a Saturday, the 29th of December, 1923, at eight o'clock in the evening.

A supernatural and very wonderful impress of grace
seemed at once to fill the whole house. Heaven was
in that little cell; the unearthly beauty of her countenance reflected something of the serenity and stability
of eternity. All remarked the majesty of the dead face,
through which shone forth as it were the Heart of Him
who had marked and chosen out her humble personality to reveal to others the designs of His Heart.

CHAPTER IV

SOON after the death of Josefa the veil of mystery surrounding her began to lift, and those among whom she had so long lived unknown began to be aware of some of the great privileges that had been granted to the humble Sister in their midst, whose last hours had been a partial revelation to them of her exceptional holiness. Nevertheless, the utmost discretion prevailed, and little was said of what had been marvellous in her life, so that the outside world remained ignorant of the nature of her gifts.

The object of this little volume is to make known in a measure some of the favours of which she was the recipient, but we wish at the outset to make it clear that in the statement of facts that follows we submit our judgment in everything to that of the Holy See, to whom alone it belongs to decide in such matters.

What stands out, and as it were stamps all in the document as of divine origin, is the impenetrable screen of obscurity and silence that enveloped Josefa throughout her years in religion; God hid her from all eyes—a fact quite unaccountable from its difficulty, surrounded as she was by a big Community of very sane and clear-sighted persons; yet not one of them—and this is quasi miraculous—so much as suspected the nature of her marvellous communications with the Sacred Heart of Our Lord, with the one exception of her religious Superiors, to whom by Our Lord's own command she submitted everything, so that all along they, and they only, knew and followed her progress along her uncharted ways.

This characteristic of humble hiddenness was willed and vigilantly safeguarded by her divine Master, so that she whom He had chosen as His confidante should remain little in her own eyes and in those of her Sisters in religion. "I have not chosen thee for what thou art," He told her again and again, "but for what thou art not, and in thee I have found where to place My power and My love."

A fortnight of absolutely unclouded bliss followed on Sister Josefa's entrance into religion. But it was only a respite, and soon Hell was let loose on her with violent and diabolic temptations, in which she seemed to founder in profound darkness. At first the assaults of the Evil One were of a normal character, but they went on gaining in strength and persistence, so that her very vocation appeared to be endangered. Never before had she experienced such fiendish attacks. "Death could not be worse," she assured her Superior. She remained, however, faithful to Rule at every point, and carried on her work undismayed. It was but the beginning of a struggle which was to continue till her death. Obediently she reiterated: "I will be faithful, yes, faithful till death."

The combat was waged without truce, till one day (she wrote): "Jesus manifested Himself to me so plainly that light and courage returned; it was the 5th of June, 1920, and that day the attacks of the Devil had been more than usually formidable. I was at adoration of the Blessed Sacrament, with all the other

Sisters, when, as I knelt there, I felt myself suddenly enveloped in a very sweet sleep. I awoke to find myself in the Sacred Wound of Our Lord's Heart. I cannot recount what passed in me then! O Jesus, my one desire is ever to love Thee and be faithful to my vocation."

In the light that surrounded her she saw the sins of all the world and offered herself to console the wounded Heart of Our Lord. She burned with a vehement longing to be united to Him, and no sacrifice seemed too great to her in her desire to be faithful to her vocation. The former darkness had melted away in the light of God, and her desolation had given place to a joy ineffable. Our Lord Himself had wrought the change. She wrote later, under obedience: "I am astounded at such goodness! O that I might love Him to delirium! I ask only two things of Him, love and gratitude to His Divine Heart . . . more than ever I recognise my weakness, still more than ever, too, I look to Him for courage and fortitude. I had never before rested in that blessed Wound—now I know where to fly for refuge in trouble—it is a place of rest, but above all of much love.

On the 29th of June, after several apparitions of the Sacred Heart, which she saw as if steeped in flames, Our divine Lord showed Himself to her in ravishing beauty. "Shortly before the Elevation of the Sacred Host at Mass," she wrote, "my eyes, even these wretched eyes, perceived the One Desired of my soul, my Lord and my God! His Heart was wrapped in ardent fire; He smiled at me gently; and whilst I was annihilated at the sight of so much beauty and light, He spoke to me in a voice both sweet and grave: 'Even as I am immolated as a Victim of love, so do I desire that thou shouldst be My victim; Love can refuse nothing.' The Sacred Heart was opened to me, never again to be closed."

We shall from now on follow Josefa in that luminous wake of grace which was to deepen and broaden till the day in which Our Lord, having accomplished His designs on her soul, called her home to hide for evermore in His Sacred Heart.

He constitutes Himself her Master and takes charge of her religious formation even in the minutest details. He instructs, He directs, He corrects, sustains and pardons her. She never knows at what moment to expect these divine visitations. Now she will find Him waiting for her at her work; again He joins her in the middle of it; He teaches her how to pray. Most unexpectedly she is aware of His presence, and again He hides from her most ardent longings. Like a flash He passes her, to chide for some lack in love's memory— He bids her tarry at His Feet to hear His behests. Sometimes it is His Cross, at another His Crown that He offers her, and with divine condescension He pillows her on His Sacred Heart or fills her with fear before the majesty of His power. He enters into the smallest details of her life as into the profoundest vicissitudes of her most secret thoughts, in each bringing light and reassurance. Untiringly the Master comes back to the groundwork of generous love . . . to its practical conclusions, obedience, fidelity, self-forgetfulness, confidence and courageous immolation of self. He ever points to the sure path of Rule, and demands obedience to it as her rampart, while His Sacred Heart is the bourne towards which she is to tend.

Frequent as these visits occasionally were, at other times they were spaced at long intervals which extended even to months. No allowance was made for mere idle enjoyment of these heavenly favours. The end for which they were granted was one of faith—and deepened in her the conviction of how great was the perfection of her calling and how profound must be the gift of self to the freedom of God.

Our Lady before long took a share in this heavenly converse: "When the glance of Jesus, my Son, is fixed on a soul, I rest my heart on it," she said to her once. These "so beautiful and so motherly" visits leave Josefa tongue-tied from sheer inability to express her feelings. The Mother of God came to her with most tender compassion and gracious kindness; to her Divine Son she left full control in this mysterious training, only making her intervention felt in moments of doubt and fear, when her terrified child needed her warnings and comfort. She prepared her for the coming of her Son, and in moments of trembling weakness she, as it were, took her by the hand and gently brought her back to the acceptance of God's Will. She taught her how to repair her failings, and how to be on her guard against the snares of the enemy. In moments of extreme peril she was there to defend her, "formidable as an army set in array."

Saint Madeleine Sophie shared the motherly cares of the Mother of God for Josefa; and in the old cloisters where she had once laboured and suffered herself she met her; or maybe she appeared to her in her cell or when she was before the Blessed Sacrament; but her presence was always reassuring, her countenance alight and ardent as in life, with the added radiance of Heaven. Josefa spoke to her with the same simplicity and trust as she was wont to do with the Superiors she loved; she listened to her advice and warnings, confided her fears and difficulties to her, relied on her word and was comforted by her kindness. She felt herself safe and her vocation secure in her proximity.

These visits do not seem to have astonished their recipient. She was too supernatural to seek the comfort they brought as such; she neither desired them nor stopped to examine them or herself too closely. She passed simply on to the lessons they were meant to convey, lessons of "a greater love" whispered to her by grace under a sensible appearance. No doubt it was Our Lord's intention, as He Himself told Josefa, to reawaken in souls belief in invisible realities; He wished to give proof in the story of her whom it was His Will so to guide, of what a loving Master can be interiorly to the soul that trusts and believes and is docile to His guidance, allowing itself to be led, bringing all troubles to His Feet, and expecting nothing outside Himself.

Simultaneously there runs through the thread of Josefa's life a trial which is a sure indication of divine action, that of opposition. It is the touchstone of the supernatural and of true virtue, and therefore could not fail to cross her path.

There were first the very formal commands of obedience, dictated by prudence, to try and test her spirit and the truth of what she saw and heard. This control was intended, in the designs of God, to bring clearly to light the detachment and obedience of the humble religious.

Josefa would then endeavour with unvarying spirit of faith and entire generosity to close the eyes of her soul and resist the overmastering dominion of the Divine. The Master had admonished her with a compelling urgency she could never forget always to obey: "I want thee to obey always, and I also shall obey." Who can tell what suffering she underwent at being led along paths that were discredited and doubted by those she most revered? How consuming the fear that gripped her that she might in very truth be mistaken and deluded, and worse, deluding others! The anguish grew in intensity, till He who alone could calm her fears bade her let it pass; detachment and humility had done their work in her soul.

More painful even than exterior opposition was the interior resistance and repugnance she experienced. Her love of common life was intense, of hard work and of all that constituted her religious life; she would, naturally speaking, so infinitely have preferred to be like everybody else, and her active, courageous disposition chafed inwardly at what she foresaw were God's designs on her future. The notes which under obedience she was compelled to write, and which she loyally coped with to the best of her ability, at times reveal the inward struggle. Not the least of her fears was an ever-present anxiety that the favours of which she was the object would in some way jeopardise her vocation or at best interfere with common life; it even happened that when Our Lord's voice was heard calling her away from her work, there arose in her soul an unaccountable distaste; chiefly, she knew, because of the account to be rendered, the divine wishes to be transmitted, and the inevitable notes to be written—yet she never shirked that which she so much dreaded.

There were other moments of sharpest anguish when her soul was storm-tossed and almost overwhelmed by the consciousness of the magnitude of the graces bestowed on her lowliness, and at such moments the arch-enemy knew well how best to torment her. Again, fear played its part: her path was so strange, so out of the common, nor could she forget the old distrust which had so alarmed her, forbidding her to pursue the track marked out for her by divine persistence— so acutely rose her painful dread, that she felt she must fly and so escape from the deception under which she was surely labouring.

When these terrible moments that so deeply disturbed her soul were past, Josefa was oftenest wont to recover her balance through the intervention of Our Lady; then with all the spontaneity of her tender love she would return to her Divine Master braced and encouraged. He granted her His forgiveness at once, as when He said to her: "My Blood washes out every stain," yet the oblation He demanded had to be made: "Josefa, tell Me again that for love of Me thou art ready to bear the Cross of My Will."

The Cross was to press yet more heavily on her weak shoulders, and opposition of another kind, much more formidable, awaited her. This was from the Evil One— he made her feel his diabolical hostility, and God seemed to allow him a free rein, so vehement was his action, which nevertheless confirmed the authenticity of the first of her supernatural graces.

Even in her postulantship Josefa had come in contact with the violence of the infernal agency attacking her. The apparition of the 5th of June had overcome the malignant powers of Hell, and as we have already recounted, she had recovered her peace of mind in the Wound of her Divine Master's Heart; and for a time she remained at peace. Our Lord was strengthening His wavering child, and at the same time giving Superiors an assurance of the divine origin of her visions, before allowing the devil an increase of power over her. She needed, indeed, all the strength and grace granted her when the moment came for a worse assault. The ordinary trials undergone by souls seem mere shadows when compared with what she had to endure; these diabolical interventions assumed a character of such vindictiveness that they appeared to be aiming at one only result—to tear Josefa away from her consecrated life as a religious, and thus ruin at one stroke God's designs, of which she was the chosen agent. Temptations, obsessions, palpable onslaughts, hand to hand contests—a veritable martyrdom ensued—traces of which she bore on her body to her dying day.

How glibly these facts can be enunciated, but what heroism was called for in bearing a combat which lasted for days and nights consecutively, and whose severity could only be guessed at by those who were witnesses of her agony, as she bravely defended her beloved vocation.

During all this time of stress Josefa carried on her ordinary work in the midst of the unsuspecting Community; only the look of suffering on her face and her halting steps betrayed something of her exhaustion. Omitting no duty, she was punctual, devoted, even-tempered, bearing her burden in silence. She met the taunts of the Evil One with the words Our Lord Himself had taught her: "Unless power were given thee from above, thou couldst do nothing against me." Her soul was maturing; threats and blows no longer scared her, but the cruel obsessions which at times darkened her mind were far harder to bear. There seemed to be in her a dual personality, and the love of the one was no longer able to master the rebellion of the other. The effect, however, was always to purify her by humiliation, to bind her closer to the Heart of God, to increase her understanding of His infinite mercy and rivet her soul in abandonment to His uncomprehended Will.

Great as these trials were, they were not the worst of her ordeal. God permitting, it seemed to her that she came into mysterious contact with Hell itself, descending into the place of fire and torments. She was able in the clear view it gave her to gauge what is meant by "a lost soul"—the full horror of separation from God—and woe of woes! she knew what it was, no longer to love God.

There is no doubt that her expiatory sufferings were saving many souls, and that Satan, who thought to triumph over her, was in reality furthering God's scheme of love in her regard.

Josefa was almost crushed by the weight of these

experiences, and she testified that all the sufferings in the world were as nothing if only thereby a soul could be saved from falling into Hell. "Such motives gave her great courage to bear pain and made her value the smallest sacrifices," for by them Jesus, who gathers them up, saves many souls from that awful fate."

Our Lady exhorted her to have ever in mind the reprobate, who, having forfeited their eternal salvation, are unable to make so much as one act of love. "It ought to excite thee to offer hourly at the throne of God the homage of thy love, that it may drown the unending clamour of their blasphemies."

There were phases of Josefa's trials that God willed to keep hidden, and these have remained an impenetrable mystery—such glimpses of their significance as were made manifest by her, show that it was on suffering that His work in her soul was founded, and the crucial ordeals through which she had to pass, were the price at which He inclined in her favour the wills of those to whose guidance on earth He had committed her, while they were the means of securing her humility.

Once indeed Jesus slept in Peter's bark, but that He now neither slumbered nor slept was proved in His divinely appointed time, for presently He commanded the waves and the sea, as He alone could do, and "there came a great calm." It was followed by His sensible Presence and ineffable consolations; but through all re-echoed the cry for souls, souls. The burden was always the same!

Josefa seems to have understood this apostolic call from childhood, for her prayer was ever world-wide;

now her Lord was Himself taking in hand the guidance of her vocation.

No sooner had she entered, than He disclosed to her His thirst for souls, bidding her share it. He gave her a clear knowledge of what He understood by "the saving of Souls" and at what price they were to be gained. He initiated her into that integral part of her vocation which is the spirit of reparation. "He showed me," she tells us in her unadorned language, "an interminable file of souls . . . all waiting for thee." Small wonder that from that day she was ever in travail and in pain for the souls thus confided to her by Our Lord. "Come," He would say eagerly to her, "come and be busy with Me about souls."

He showed her how to use the smallest occasions of her daily life for that end, and impressed on her the value of a day spent in union with His Sacred Heart.

For these dear souls He bids her offer up her prayers with Him, and taught her how to sacrifice His redeeming Blood and His Heart, how to identify herself with the sublime Sacrifice of the Mass and of the Tabernacle, wherein He offers Himself as a Victim for the salvation of the whole world.

He pleaded with her for costly penances and mortifications, and (subject always to obedience) she is prodigal of them, unmindful of the claims of nature.

Finally He selects her as a victim and mysteriously associates her in the sufferings of His Passion. "Wilt thou carry My Cross?" He often asks her; and carry it she does for hours at a time, weighed down by the burden; the Crown of Thorns encircles her head, making rest impossible, while an acute pain in her side associates her with the thrust of the lance which transpierced the Sacred Heart. Yet she goes on with her daily work, and at night especially is on guard, lest He should summon her.

Once in particular He appeared and bade her rise. "Take My Cross, Nails and Crown of Thorns . . . all My treasures . . . for thou art My Chosen One and gladly I entrust them to thy keeping . . . guard them safely till I return, I go to seek souls." Flames burst from the open Wound in the Divine Heart. "Come," Our Lord continued. . . . "All must learn to know and love Me; come, together we shall draw them into My Wounds, and while I seek them do thou carry My Cross . . . when I have found them I shall return and take it from thee once more."

Great as these physical sufferings were, they cannot compare with those of the soul. Our Lord gave Josefa a share in the agony which drew from Him the great cry: "My God, My God, why hast Thou forsaken Me?" But at once He is at hand, sustaining her, and whispering the oft-repeated lesson: the supreme value of souls; He reminds her why she has been specially chosen. As an appeal to her sacrificing love: "Never forget that My Chosen Ones are to be victims with Me for the world." This collaboration in the work of Redemption henceforward filled her days and nights; the thought of souls was never absent from her mind and she carried out literally Our Lord's prophetic words to her: "I shall live in thee, and thou shalt live for souls."

It was on the 16th of July, 1922, that, victorious over the enemy of souls, Josefa at length offered herself to God in the fulness of her faith and love by the emission of her vows.

We know something of what passed between her and her Lord on that long desired day: He appeared to her, she saw His glowing Heart and Its gaping Wound; "He was divinely beautiful, and drew me gently into It," she related afterwards.

Then she heard His voice: "Now I shall keep thee for ever in this prison, for from all eternity I have loved thee; to-day thou art for ever Mine—even thou, Josefa! Labour for Me, I shall labour for thee; thy interests are Mine, and Mine are thine." And He continued caressingly: "Have I not been faithful to thee?" And with might and majesty He added: "Now I begin My great work."

CHAPTER V

"BY their fruits ye shall know them," Our Blessed Lord had once said to His disciples, and the principle holds good for all that is supernatural in virtue here below.

To Josefa (who was unconscious of any perplexity in her regard by Superiors) Our Lord said: "No one need ask Me for a sign; thou thyself shalt be My sign." The reply justified itself for them, who, secretly confused by the strangeness of the ways in which Josefa was being led, asked for a sign of the authenticity of the marvels that had become a matter of daily occurrence. Her virtue was proof, were any needed, that all came from God.

It showed itself first and foremost in her childlike simplicity. She was one of those singleminded, lowly souls that truly ravish the Heart of God, and to whom He revealed His secrets. There was in her a total absence of self-consciousness, a confiding simplicity, a straightforward spontaneity, which were very striking. There was nothing "precious" about her devotion, or anything in the least complicated in her attitude of mind. Her faith was of too firm a texture to admit of exaggerations or fantastic imaginings. She went straight as an arrow to God.

It was this simplicity, innate and baffling, that engendered her effortless approach to the divine, and enabled her to cope with trials of which she did not so much as suspect the gravity and bearing, and that, without losing her hold on what was ordinary and normal in daily intercourse.

Her manner of giving an account of herself to Superiors was devoid of anything in the nature of pretentiousness; it was as direct as it was matter-of-fact. When H. Ex. Mgr. de Durfort, Bishop of Poitiers, saw her and repeatedly spoke with her, what struck him most was precisely this deferential, ingenuous and candid simplicity, which made the singleness of her aim and purpose so evident. God was all she wanted—even in her writings and notes the artlessness and limpidity of her soul were apparent.

Humility and charity, the two characteristics of the Heart of Jesus, recognised by the Church as peculiarly those of the Foundress St. Madeleine Sophie, were likewise distinctive of Josefa's virtue.

There was something grave and mature about her which was the result of the lowly opinion she had of herself; though proud and vivacious by nature, which naturally made acts of these virtues difficult to her, Our Lord seems to have provided her with the occasions (so frequent withal in religious life) by which she might practise love in the smallest details and by the difficulty she experienced in so doing become sensible of her own weakness, so as genuinely to judge herself to be the last in the house.

Other ways were not wanting of gauging the sincerity of her humility. Lowliness and self-sacrifice, both a habit with her, were the logical outcome of her conviction of her own nothingness, and the source of many conflicts. It had been an heroic act of submission to God's Will that she had accepted to enter

on a course so opposed to her natural inclinations;
hence each step she took increased in her detachment
from her own views and humble trust in authority.

Her humility was all the more authentic that its
outward manifestation was one of charity, a charity so
supernatural that it bound her every day more closely
to the Heart of Jesus.

A humility less real might have taken advantage
of her exceptional favours to stand aside from common life, wrapped in a kind of self-complacency;
but there was no trace of this in Josefa. The more
the Sacred Heart made her the confidante of His
secrets and filled her with His spirit, the greater became
the evidence of her sweet charity. The closer her contact with the intangible and the more she was steeped
in things divine, the more simply helpful and kindly
she grew towards others, her interest in them, her gift
of self and her ready prayers on their behalf never
failing them. The whole world, nothing less, to be
gained for Christ was the sole boundary of her horizon;
yet no tiny service was allowed to escape her watch-
ful attentions for each and all. Over and above the
world of souls, and of her community, there was plenty
of space in her heart with which to love God's beautiful
nature—the birds, flowers and insects; the starry sky;
she embraced them all in her broad, strong, yet
simple and naïve affection.

Obedience in the long run is the one touchstone of
virtue, and one ever stressed by Our Lord Himself.
The witnesses of her daily life certify how supernatural
she was in its exercise. The control over her actions
and spirit to which she submitted was perfect: a sub-

mission both of judgment and heart. She never expressed a wish, had no attachment to one way of acting rather than another, and never reasoned at decisions taken in her regard. She simply and wholly submitted herself to the line of conduct prescribed—and so disengaged was she from self that she refrained even from comment on the graces she had received, and much less expressed any sort of complaisance.

The written notes, which were such a burden to her, she never failed to take, nor did she ever ask to read them again. She just handed everything over to her Superiors.

This she had learned from Our Lord's own mouth; He demanded of her complete dependence on authority. "I have drawn thee to My Heart that obedience may be thy very breath; know this, My Child, that should I ask one thing of thee and thy Superiors another, I prefer thee to obey them rather than Me."

One of the first obediences laid upon her was that she should never answer her heavenly visitants without having first obtained permission. It was Our Lord's own wish, and He watched over its observance. "Go and ask leave," He would say to her. He Himself explained to her how far and in what degree she was to be docile and pliant, and as it were transparent in her openness with Superiors. Again and again He came back to the point, impressing on Josefa the importance of this paramount virtue of religious life. "Seek Me in thy Superiors. Listen to their admonitions as if they fell from My lips; I am in them for thy guidance." Josefa adhered faithfully to this line of conduct.

Her love for the Rule and of common life played a conspicuous part in defending her against the snares of the devil and against illusion. She loved both, and proved it by her generous fidelity; many a time her love of common life made her choose rather to follow it than obey a precept laid on her by Our Lord Himself, unless, of course, He gave her a clear assurance of His Divine Will. People little suspected sometimes how heroic were the acts of courage and will by which she defied the Evil One, threatening her with dire consequences if she obeyed the first sound of the bell, for instance; yet, though she dreaded the conflict and moral agony involved, love made her venture and dare to brave the fiend. (One has only to remember what an antagonist she was up against, and what his savage power.)

Finally, we may add one last proof of the divine origin of Josefa's way of life in the perfect *concordance* between the teaching she received from the Sacred Heart of Our Lord and the Rule she so loved, and the spirit bequeathed by the Foundress, St. Madeleine Sophie, to her daughters. That spirit is one of love and generosity, of reparation and zeal, and should be the distinctive mark of every member of the Society— Spouses, victims and apostles. Josefa only gained in this spirit from the teaching of her divine Instructor; and greatly as she valued it, she never balanced its importance with that of her vocation, the direction of obedience, and the security of the Rule.

And so Our Lord's words: "Thou shalt be thyself My sign," came true; day by day and hour by hour, in every tiny detail of her religious life, enveloped in silence and obscurity, the unsuspected intensity of her love was hidden in her generous self-oblation. There were, notwithstanding, days, nay—months, when obedience, love of duty, courage and submission to God's Will, Faith and abandonment to His divine ruling, required sheer heroism on Josefa's part. How often the passive witnesses of her superhuman struggles and anguish at times were amazed at her gallant fight, at the fidelity, liberty of spirit and overmastering grace displayed in the conduct of this simple child of the people, so unconscious of the grandeur of her destiny and giving such unequivocal signs of genuine virtue.

The story of her short life is about to close: death came as it had been predicted in the first place by Our Lady in December of 1921. The exact date and the accompanying circumstances were revealed in due course by Our Lord Himself, and Josefa warned her Superiors that she would not see the close of the year 1923.

The Master of life and death came to summon His beloved Child and conclude His "great work" in her on the date and in the manner predicted. This we shall see in the next chapter.

CHAPTER VI

Soon after Sister Josefa had made her vows Our Lord made it evident to her that He wished her to become the agent of His love for souls. He had already many times made her aware of His divine intentions in her regard: "I shall make use of thee to carry out My purpose, in spite of thy lowliness and nothingness," and again: "Thou art to become the apostle of My loving-kindness and mercy."

The prospect filled Josefa's heart with fear, but Our Lord reassured her: "I will what thou willest not, fear not, only love." And on another occasion: "I can do what thou canst not do; keep My words in thy memory and believe in them—the sole object of My Heart is to take thine into Its custody, entirely to possess thee and to make of thine incompetence and infirmity a channel of mercy for souls who will be saved through thee. . . . I do not employ thee for any merit of thine, but that it should become evident that My Power can use wretched and feeble instruments."

On the 6th of August, 1922, a few weeks after her vows, when the Novena of the Assumption was about to begin, Our Lord appeared to her: "Come," He said, drawing her gently to His Heart, "now that thy wretchedness and nothingness are known to thee, My words that I will speak shall never pass away." "I answered," wrote Josefa in her notes, "that I greatly feared to be entrusted with so great a work, because of all the evil I am capable of. Immediately there came forth from His Heart flames of fire, and with tenderest accents He answered me: "Josefa, My Chosen One, begin this work hand in hand with My Mother; she will give thee courage." There flashed before her eyes a vision of what the future held in store for her, and again she heard the Divine voice: "It matters not at all that thou art so little and worthless, for I Myself will do all, and none of My words shall pass away."

With tenderest charity Our Lord comforted her with renewed assurances that He would teach her His secrets, making her a living example of His Mercy, because "If I have such loving predilection for thee, who art of no account, what would I not do for souls more magnanimous than thine?"

From that time on the work of love began to be unfolded to her; apparently Our Lord's plan was a twofold one, which we can sum up, "in order to admire every detail," as He Himself said to Josefa. From the lessons of His Sacred Heart, from the guidance given to Josefa, as well as from the graces she received, we gather first that it was His Will to accentuate the main doctrines of Faith, reminding souls of them as divine precepts.

They were: First, the Sovereign Dominion of the Creator over the creature. Second, His Providence that never errs. Third, the actuality of grace in every soul. Fourth, the value of vital union with Him. Fifth, participation in the merits of Jesus Christ. Sixth, the Communion of Saints. Seventh, the reality of Hell.

THE SOVEREIGN DOMINION OF THE CREATOR OVER THE CREATURE, and the utter dependence on His Will that He looks for: "Never forget My claims over thee, let Me do with thee whatsoever I will . . . let Me act in thee . . . let Me exert My power . . . let Me dispose of thee, leave thyself entirely in My hands," are words that occur again and again.

Josefa's whole history shows a PROVIDENCE THAT NEVER ERRS. "My wish is that thou shouldst let thy littleness be led and guided by My Fatherly Hand, which is infinitely wise and strong. . . . I will manage thee in a manner befitting My glory and the good of souls. . . . Fear nothing, for I watch over thee with jealous care, even as the tenderest of mothers watches over her infant." Magnanimous and divine fidelity, able to say to each of us in every change of circumstance: "Never have I broken My word."

THE ACTUALITY OF GRACE IN EVERY SOUL, on which foundation rests its incorporation in the Divine Life. "I live in her . . . it is My good pleasure to be one with her. . . ." In return, He pleads with her never to leave Him . . . to consult Him, to beg all graces from Him, and, above all, to clothe herself in Him, and hide for evermore in His life. "The more thou shalt disappear, the more I shall become thy life." The words of St. Paul are a true commentary: "I live, no, not I, but Christ liveth in me."

THE IMMENSE VALUE OF THIS VITAL UNION WITH HIM, transmuting our poor activities into the pure gold of the supernatural. Many a time Our Lord showed Josefa in an obvious manner what her actions, when united to His, realised in love. He willed her to

reanimate in souls the happiness that lies in believing
in the wealth thus brought within their power. "How
many souls will gain new courage when they realise
the value of ordinary actions when united to Mine?"

We here touch on a truth which is, as it were, the
very nucleus of His teaching, i.e., our PARTICIPATION
IN THE INFINITE MERITS OF CHRIST. Constantly Our
Lord comes back on the power possessed by a baptised
soul over the treasures of Redemption.

When He pleads with Josefa "to fill up what is wanting to His Passion," to make reparation for a sinful
world and to satisfy God's Justice, it is always "With
Him, by Him and in Him." "My Heart is all thine;
take It and with It make reparation."

There followed from the divine lips words of immense
power over the Heart of His Father, which it was
Josefa's privilege to hear and which she has transmitted to us: "Father, good, holy and merciful! receive
the Blood of Thy Son . . . His Wounds . . . His Heart . . .
look upon His pierced Head . . . do not allow His
Precious Blood to have been shed in vain . . . remember
that we are still in the season of mercy rather than in
that of justice."

THE COMMUNION OF SAINTS forms, as it were, the
background of the picture in the texture of whose
canvas we discern Josefa's supernatural vocation,
on which is painted her life-story. Our Lady Media-
trix of all graces and Mother of Mercy has her own
central place in this marvellous exchange of graces and
of merits between the Church Triumphant, the Church
Militant and the Church Suffering. Josefa, a tiny
and insignificant member, is made cognisant by Him

how great is the repercussion in the world of spirits, of fidelity, sacrifice, suffering and prayer.

One spot alone escapes from the current of love that issues from the Heart of God: HELL; THE DOGMA OF ETERNAL PUNISHMENT so often contested or merely passed over in silence and ignored in these days of waning faith, is divinely and luminously vindicated. No one who, like ourselves, has witnessed the traces of fire imprinted on the garments, nay, on the very members of Josefa, could doubt the existence of an infernal Power fiercely antagonistic to Christ and His Kingdom. In Josefa how frail a barrier was opposed by God to the violence of Hell.

Over and above these doctrinal teachings, so valuable in themselves, the direct message of the Heart of Jesus is one of Love and Mercy. On a certain day Josefa asked her divine Master to tell her what was the meaning of "The great work" He so often alluded to, He replied: "Dost thou not know what My work is? It is LOVE. . . . I intend to use thee to manifest yet more the love of My Heart. The words and desires that through thee I convey to others will excite the zeal of many souls and prevent the loss of others, and all must know that the Mercy of My Heart is inexhaustible. . . . I thirst to make all men listen to My appeal of Love. It is true that I have no real need of thee—but, Josefa, My Chosen One, let Me manifest Myself to souls through thee yet once again."

During the two years that followed Our Lord continued to make known His great designs, by means of Josefa, who for the most part received these communications in the little cell, to which He summoned her.

There, kneeling under the statue of Our Lady, she renewed her vows (an act of obedience which many a time saved her from being taken in by the snares of the Evil One) and listened to the Voice which told her Its secrets.

Fragments of these disclosures are recorded in the chapters that follow, but we first sum them up in a few words, to make the plan of the whole stand out more clearly.

"Deus caritas est" is the burden of His teaching and the testimony He renders to His Heavenly Father.

Through the new evidence of the love of His Heart Jesus desires to obtain from men, not only a return of love, but the response of utter trustfulness, which He values as its true proof and the expression of its sincerity.

His purpose is to attract souls and rebuild them in faith and trust in His merciful goodness, both of which are so little understood or believed in.

To fervent souls He wishes to impart greater security, by deepening their knowledge of His love and through them, imparting it to others.

He wants His appeal to awaken the tepid, to lift up the fallen and satisfy yearnings all the world over; so ardent are these desires, so positive their assertion, that none can be insensible to them.

At the same time He reminds His followers that in accordance with His Providence, His plans depend in a measure on their free co-operation.

This co-operation is essential for all who are capable of comprehending its importance and the ardour of His divine expectations. "When souls have once understood My designs, let them spare neither trouble, effort nor suffering."

It was in this sense that Josefa understood the yearnings of the Sacred Heart, the effect of which deep understanding eventually brought about the consummation of her earthly pilgrimage.

On the 9th of June, 1923, Our Lord appeared to her during her thanksgiving, with His Heart all aflame, and in response to her prayer that He would make Himself known to the world He said: "Fear not, Josefa; thou knowest what happens when a volcano is in eruption? So great is the force of the flowing lava that it is capable of removing mountains and destroying them. Do men, then, need to be told that a devastating power has been unloosed? Such will be the strength of My words, accompanied by grace—that even the most obdurate will be conquered by Love."

May this promise find its accomplishment to-day, and the treasures of the Divine Heart riven for us be poured forth.

PART II

THE MESSAGE

PART II

"I WANT the world to know My Heart, and that men should come to the knowledge of My Love, for as yet they know not what I have done for them. For this do I come, to tell them that in vain do they seek for happiness elsewhere; they will never find it but in Me.

"My appeal is for all—for the just, for sinners, for the wise and for the ignorant, for masters and learners. To all I say: If you want happiness, seek it in Me— if peace, I am Peace—I am Mercy and Love.

"Love must be the sun to enlighten and the heat to reanimate souls; I want all the world to recognise in Me a God of Mercy and of Love.

"All men must know how ardently I long to forgive and save them . . . the most outcast, even, need not have fear! Neither let the guilty fly from Me! Let them all come, for as a loving Father, I stand with open arms to bestow on them life, peace and true happiness."

* *

"MY words are for all the world; let them hearken to them:

"A Father once had an only Son.

"They were rich and powerful, served by devoted dependants and surrounded by all in life that makes for honour, happiness and pleasure, and there was nothing, either person or thing, wanting to their good fortune. The Son was all in all to the Father and the Father to his Son, and each found in the other perfect contentment, not so as to exclude others, for the smallest mishap befalling them found an echo of tender pity in hearts so noble and generous.

"Now it came to pass that one of the servants of this good Master fell ill. The danger increased, and the only hope of saving his life lay in the application of powerful remedies and most careful nursing.

"But this servant lay at home, poor and lonely, at which the Master taking alarm, felt he must not be left deserted, which would be to condemn him to death, a thing unthinkable. What was to be done? True, a fellow servant could be sent to minister to him; but as it would be done for gain rather than for love it gave no assurance against possible neglect.

"So, moved with compassion, the Master calls His Son, and communicates his anxiety to him,—the man will die—the most attentive care unremittingly bestowed alone can save him.

"Like Father, like Son! The offer to go himself to succour the dying man is at once made—He will spare neither trouble, fatigue nor night-watches until the man's health is fully re-established.

"The Father accepts His Son's offer, and willingly allows him to take on the likeness of a servant, that He may serve him who is his slave.

"Many months go by—months of anxious watching by the sick-bed, till at length health is restored, thanks to his devoted patience and kindness. And what of the servant? With a heart overflowing with gratitude for all that has been done for him, he asks what he can do to make return for such marvellous charity.

" ' Go seek out my Father, and with restored health offer thyself to become his faithful follower in return for his liberality.'

"Overwhelmed by his obligations, the man stands in humble gratitude before his Benefactor and proffers his services gratis for ever; what need has he of remuneration with such a Master, who has treated him not as a servant but as a son?

"This parable is but a pale image of the love I bear to mankind, and of the loving return I look for from them. At least it will let them know what are the feelings of My Heart towards them."

* *

GOD created man out of pure love. He placed him on the earth in circumstances that insured his happiness until the day of everlasting bliss should dawn for him. To have a right to this felicity he is bound to keep the sweet and wise laws laid down by his Maker.

Man, unfaithful to this law, fell grievously sick; sin was committed by our first parents and all mankind, their descendants, contracted this guilt and lost their right to the perfect beatitude promised them by God; henceforward pain, suffering and death became their lot.

Now, God is sufficient for Himself; He has no need of any other to share His bliss. Infinite is His glory, and nothing can diminish it.

Infinite in power, He is also infinite in goodness, hence He will not allow man, created out of love, to perish; instead, He meets the grave evil of sin with a remedy infinite in price: one of the Divine Persons of the Blessed Trinity, by assuming human nature, will repair in a godlike manner the malignity of the fall.

The Father gives His Son, the Son Incarnate relinquishes in His Manhood the glory that should be His—not as an all-powerful Lord and Master, but poor and in subjection, as one who serves.

The life led by Him on earth is known to you all.

*   *

"You know how from the first moment of My Incarnation I submitted to all human afflictions.

"It was through love that I was born in the rigour of winter's cold, poor and stripped of all comfort. In My Childhood I endured hunger, poverty and persecution.

"It was love that made Me spend thirty years in complete obscurity, in hiddenness and labour, subject to the will of My Mother and My foster-father.

"In this life of labour, how often humiliation and contempt were meted out to the carpenter's son—how often after a hard day's work we were found to have hardly earned sufficient to support us. And this I continued for thirty long years.

"Later, foregoing the sweet company of My Mother, I devoted Myself to the task of making My Heavenly Father known. I ever taught men that God is love.

"I went about doing good, both to bodies and souls, for to the sick I gave back health, the dead I raised to life; and to souls? . . . Ah! to souls I restored indeed . . . liberty; that liberty which they had lost through sin, and I opened to them the gates of their everlasting home—Heaven."

"Then came the hour when it pleased God that His

Son should shed His Blood, and surrender life itself.
And how did He die?"

"It was not surrounded by friends, acclaimed as a
benefactor, that He willed to die! Beloved souls, He
Who had come to set man free was cast bound into
prison; He was ill-treated and calumniated. He Who
had come to bring peace to the world became an object
of inexorable savagery; He Who had taught men to
love one another died a victim of their hatred on a
cross, between two thieves—contemned, abandoned,
abject and despoiled of everything.

"It was thus that He surrendered Himself for Man's
salvation.

"It was thus that He accomplished the work for
which He had voluntarily left the Father's glory. Man
was sick and wounded, and the Son of God came down
to him. He did by His death not only restore to fallen
man his life, but He earned for him both strength and
power to acquire in this life the treasures of eternal
beatitude."

* *

How did man respond to so many favours?

Did he, like the grateful servant, offer to serve his
Master gratis and have no other interests but His?

Let us examine and distinguish between different
ways in which man responded to his God.

* *

"Some have truly known Me, and urged by love have
ardently desired to make an entire sacrifice of themselves to My service, which is that of My Father. They
begged Him to show them what was the greatest

thing they could do in His service, and My Father answered thus:

"'Leave all things, surrender all your possessions, and having surrendered *self*, come, and follow Me and do whatsoever I shall tell you.'

"Others, moved by all the Son of God has done for their salvation, with good-will offer themselves to Him, endeavouring to make a return for His goodness to them by working for His interests alone, without, however, giving up all things completely.

"To these My Father says: 'Observe the Law which the Lord your God has given you; keep His commandments, and erring neither to the right nor to the left, live in the peace which belongs to servants that are faithful.

"There are others again who have little comprehension of God's great love, yet they have an upright will and live under the Law though with little love— they follow rather an instinctive attraction for good, left in their hearts by grace.

"These are *not* willing servants; they have *not* offered themselves to obey God's Law; yet, being of good-will, they easily accept His yoke when occasion offers to serve Him.

"There are yet others who submit to their God not through love, but through self-interest, and only to the extent of not endangering the final reward promised to those who keep His Law.

"And are there no others outside these groups found to offer God their service? And others who, ignorant of the great love of which they are the object, make no response to all the Son of God has suffered for them?

"Alas! Many indeed know and . . . contemn and despise it; but a far greater number are entirely ignorant of it."

For each of these Jesus Christ Himself has a word of love.

*   *

"I will speak in the first place to those who know Me not: My sons, who from infancy have lived apart from your Father, . . . come; I will tell you why you do not know Me . . . for once you realise the affection I bear you, you will not resist My love.

"Is it not often the case that those who are brought up far from their parents have little affection for them; but when by chance the sweet love of father or mother is revealed to them, it awakens a keener appreciation in them than it does in those who have never left home.

"To you who not only do not love, but hate and persecute Me, I say: 'Why this hatred? What have I done to deserve persecution at your hands?'

"There are many who have never asked themselves this question—to-day when I ask it, they will perhaps reply . . . 'I know not.'

"Behold I will answer for you:

*   *

"If from childhood you have never known Me, it is because no one has ever taught you about Me; and as you grew up nature also was developing in you: love of pleasure and enjoyment, a longing for wealth and freedom. . . .

"Then came the day when first you heard of Me, and how to live according to My Will; that to do so you must love and bear with your neighbour, respect his rights and his goods and gain a mastery over your own nature; in a word, live subject to a law. Hitherto, subject only to your own natural inclinations, if not to your passions, not even knowing of what law there was 'question', to you, I say, is it to be wondered at that you should protest, should wish to enjoy life, to be free—to want to be a law unto yourself?

"In this lies the cause of your hatred and persecution of Me. But I, your Father, love you, and even as I see your blind revolt My Heart is filled with tenderness for you.

"So the years during which you led this life sped by, and they were perhaps many.

"I can to-day no longer contain My love for you! And the sight of you at war with your best Friend compels Me to enlighten you as to who I am.

*   *

"I AM Jesus, which name signifies Saviour! Why else are My Hands transfixed by nails which fasten them to a Cross on which for thy sake I died? My feet are wounded, My Heart wide open, riven by the lance after death. Thus do I stand before thee, that thou mayst know Who I am and who thou art.

"I am thy God and thy Father, thy Creator and thy Saviour. Thou art My creature, My son, bought at the price of My life and Heart's Blood, shed to free thee from slavery and the tyranny of sin.

"Thou hast a soul, great and immortal, destined for eternal happiness, a will capable of all good, a heart made both to give and receive affection.

"The thirst for happiness and love can never be appeased by earthly and fleeting gains, which will always leave thee hungry and unsatisfied. Perpetual conflict, sadness, anxiety and affliction will still be thy portion.

"If thou art poor and hast to earn a living, the miseries of life will embitter thee; thou wilt hate thy employers and mayst even wish them ill, that like thyself they may experience the hard grind of daily toil.

"Fatigue, disgust, nay, even despair will weigh heavily on thy spirit, for the way is a rough one and in the end we have to die.

"Oh! how great are these calamities when viewed from a human standpoint! But I come to show thee life under a different aspect.

"All you who are deprived of this world's goods and obliged to labour for your daily bread, reflect that you are not slaves, but created for the freedom of eternity.

"All you whose craving for affection is unsatisfied, remember that you are created to love that which is eternal, not that which passes with time.

"All who love their homes and labour to support their families and provide them with comforts and happiness, forget not that death will one day sever every tie, but only for a time.

"You who serve a master, and owe him respect and love, and care of his interests through hard work and fidelity, forget not that he is your master only for the short span of a lifetime—how soon it will pass away and lead you to an Eternity that is unending.

"Your soul, created by a loving Father, Who bears you a limitless and eternal affection, shall find one day, in the place of a beatitude He has prepared for you, the final answer to all its aspirations.

"There every labour shall be rewarded.

"There all who have been parted in this life shall be reunited to their loved ones. Oh, how great is the bliss that awaits you!"   *   *

"Perhaps you will answer Me: 'I have no Faith, nor do I believe in a future happiness.'

"Have you no Faith? Then why do you persecute Me? Why rebel against My laws? Why war against those who love Me? And since you desire peace for yourself, why not grant it to others?

"You do not believe in a future life? Tell Me are you absolutely satisfied and do you never feel a yearning for that which it is not possible to obtain here below?

"If, after seeking for enjoyment you succeed in obtaining it, does it satisfy you?

"If you pursue riches and succeed in acquiring them, very soon you will weary of them.

"None of these things will fill your life, and you will never obtain all that your heart desires here below. That which you yearn for is peace, not the peace of this world, but that of the children of God; and how do you expect to find it in the midst of rebellion?

"That is why I have come to show you where true peace and happiness are to be found, and where to slake the thirst which consumes you.

"Do not rebel when I tell you that all these things are to be found in accomplishing My Law. Fear not, for My Law is not a tyranny, it is LOVE. A law of love, because I am your God, and your Father."
     *   *

"You know that in a well-regulated army discipline must be maintained, just as in a household there are established customs to be observed; so in the great family of Jesus Christ there must be law and order, albeit a law of love.

"Listen while I explain this Law to you, and what manner of Heart it is that imposes it on you—a Heart that you know not, and so cruelly wound. You seek Me to administer death, while I seek you to impart life. Which of us two will prevail? And will you so harden yourself against Me as not to yield to One who has laid down His life for you and given you all His love?

"In the order of nature sons are not recognised as such unless they bear their father's name; so My sons bear the name of Christian given them in Baptism. All ye who bear this name are My sons, and as such have a right to your Father's estate.

"Well I know that I do not possess your love, nor do you know Me, for you detest and persecute Me. On My part I love you with an infinite tenderness, and I intend you to have a share in the heritage which is yours by right.

"Hearken to Me, consider how little I require of you, and what you are asked to do in order to acquire the benefits I offer you.

"Believe in My love and in My mercy!

"You have sinned against Me; I forgive you.

"You have persecuted Me; I love you.

"You have wounded Me both by word and deed; still I wish to do you good and make you share all My treasures.

"Do not imagine that I am ignorant of your state of soul. I know that My grace has been despised, nay, even My Sacraments profaned by you, perhaps. Yet you have from Me a full pardon."

"If, then, you would be happy in this world and secure your eternal salvation, do as I shall tell you:

"If you are poor in this world's goods, perform your duty in all subjection, even though it be an inescapable obligation; and forget not that I, too, lived for thirty years in subjection to the self-same Law, for I was needy and poor.

"Do not consider your masters as tyrants; banish all hatred from your hearts; never wish them ill; but further their interests and be faithful to them.

"If, however, you possess this world's goods and employ workers and servants, be fair to them in all your dealings; pay them a just wage, and show them both pity and kindness, for they, too, have immortal souls, and if you abound in wealth, it is not for your sole comfort and enjoyment, but that you may wisely administer it and practise charity to your neighbour. Both employer and employed must accept the law of labour with submission, acknowledging a Supreme Being over all created things, Who is both your God and your Father.

"As GOD He demands of you the accomplishment of His Divine Will.

"As your FATHER He asks you to accept His Commandments in a spirit of filial piety.

"Thus, having spent a week in the pursuit of work, business or sport, He claims but one half-hour that you may fulfil your Sunday duty. Is this excessive?

"Go, then, to your Father's House, where day and night He awaits your coming, and as Sundays and Holydays recur, give Him the homage of this half-hour by assisting at Love's Banquet, that is, Holy Mass.

"Tell Him all your troubles: all about your families, children, affairs and aspirations . . . lay at His Feet your sorrows, difficulties and sufferings. . . . Believe in the interest with which He hearkens to your prayer.

"You may perhaps say to Me: 'I have not entered a church for so many years that I have forgotten how to hear Mass.' Do not be afraid on that account, come —spend this half-hour with Me; your conscience will tell you what to do, and be docile to its voice . . . open your soul wide to grace, and it will inspire you—gradually it will teach you how to act in a given circumstance, how to treat with your family, what to do in regard to your affairs . . . how to bring up your children, love those who depend on you, and honour those in authority over you. . . . It may make you feel that such and such a concern must be given up, such a friendship relinquished, or such a risky companion avoided. . . . Again, that an individual who is distasteful to you should be cultivated; or it may put in your mind to sever your connection with some person you feel drawn to and whose advice is doing you harm. Only give grace a chance, and gradually its power will grow stronger in you, for just as evil increases insensibly, once it is given in to, so will each new grace prepare your soul for a still greater one. If you listen to My voice and let grace act, its influence will steadily increase as time goes on; light will grow in your soul, peace envelop you; and the reward is bliss eternal.

* *

"MAN was not created to live for ever here below. He was made for Eternity. If, then, he is immortal, he should live for that which will never die, not for the passing things of time.

"Youth, wealth, wisdom, human glory will all end with this life—God only will endure for ever.

"It is due to the decay of Faith that nations are in perpetual conflict with one another, and that hatred separates man from man. Only let faith reign once more over the world and peace and charity will return to it.

"Faith is not against civilization and progress; the more it is rooted in individuals and peoples, the more wisdom and learning increase, for God is Infinite in wisdom and knowledge; wherever Faith is completely lacking, peace, civilization and true progress likewise vanish . . . and in their place come enmities, clash of opinions, class wars, rebellion of passions against duty . . . and all that is noble in humanity is exchanged for revolt, insubordination and warfare.

"Do but let yourselves be guided by Faith, and you will be free; live by Faith, and you will escape eternal death.

"Let all men know that My Heart is ever on the quest for them, longs for them, waits, and is consumed with desire to draw them all, all, to Itself, that It may pardon them.

"I ask nothing better than to absolve erring souls, to pardon nations, to reign over all wills and peoples of the earth.

"Mine is to wipe out the ingratitude of men by an abundance of mercies; Mine by forgiveness, to begin a reign of peace and love.

"I am Wisdom! Joy! Peace!

"I am Mercy, I am Love!"

AN APPEAL TO SOULS

"I AM Love! My Heart is unable to confine to itself the flame that consumes It.

"I love souls so dearly that I gave My life for them.

"It is this love that keeps Me imprisoned in the Tabernacle. For nigh twenty centuries I have dwelt there, veiled under the species of Bread, hidden night and day in the small white Host; and there I bear with patience, neglect, solitude, contempt and blasphemies—all out of love. Outrages, too, and sacrilege.

"For the same motive I instituted the Sacrament of Penance, that I might forgive them—not once or twice . . . but as often as they need it to recover grace. There I tarry, expecting their coming, longing to wash away their sins—not in water, but in My very Blood.

"How often in the course of ages I have, in one way or another, made known My love, and shown mankind how ardently I desire their salvation, revealing My Heart to them. For many souls this devotion has been as light diffused over all the earth, and by its means those who labour to gain souls to My service have been enabled to do so.

* *

"IF I long for love in response to My own, I still desire something more; I want them all to have confidence in My Mercy, to expect all good things from My clemency, and that they should never doubt My readiness to forgive.

"I am your God, a God of love! Your Father, compassionate, never harsh—infinitely holy and infinitely wise, Who knoweth what is in man and inclineth towards human frailty and infirmity with divine pity.

"How tenderly I welcome those who after a first fall come to Me for pardon . . . and should they sin again, nay even often, I will forgive them a million million times; love never wearies—and I will wash them in My Blood and blot out every stain from first to last.

"Never shall I tire of repentant sinners, nor cease hoping to see them at My Feet, and all the more, the greater their distress!

"Does not a father love a sick child with a special affection? His solicitude and attentions increase in proportion to its wants. So does the bounty of My Heart, pour out compassion and mercy with greater abundance on sinners than on the just man.

* *

"THIS is the lesson I desire above all to inculcate: that My Heart's compassion is simply inexhaustible. Let the cold and indifferent know that as a vehement flame I will consume them in love. To devout and saintly souls I would be 'the Way', that, making great strides in perfection, they may safely reach the harbour of eternal felicity. To consecrated priests and religious, My elect and chosen ones, I ask once more all their love, and that they should never, never doubt Mine, and, above all, that they should trust Me implicitly. What is easier than reliance on My Heart?

"I shall make people understand that My first work in their souls has no other foundation than their own nothingness and frailty; and there begins the first link of the chain of love, which I prepare for them from all eternity.

"They shall learn to what lengths this Heart of Mine can go in love and pardon. I can discern their deep, radical desire to please, comfort and glorify Me— but when they fail through weakness, it honours and consoles My Heart to see them humbly acknowledge their defects; I will easily overcome their frailties. . . . Am I not able to provide for all their deficiencies?

"Their very weakness of purpose is used by Me to give life to many souls that have lost it.

"There is no limit to My mercy and love to fallen souls. I long to forgive . . . it is My rest and repose to pardon. I ever await their coming; let nothing discourage them; only let them throw themselves into My arms, banishing all fear; am I not their Father?

"Some do not sufficiently realise all they might do to attract souls to Me, especially those who are plunged in ignorance of My longing to bestow true life upon them.

"To thee, Josefa, I will teach the secrets of My love, and thou wilt be a living proof of My mercy; for if I bear towards thee who of thyself art of no account, a predilection and love so great, what would I not do for other and more generous souls?

"To how many souls life will be given back through

My words to Thee! How many will take courage when they realise the fruit of their efforts. Through a small act of generosity, patience, or poverty, graces that will save a soul can be stored up. In every act of man it is not the deed itself which is of consequence to Me, but the intention; the smallest acts prompted by love are transmuted into merit and give immense comfort to My Heart! For to the least I assign a divine significance and all I ask is love. Yes, love alone do I seek—love alone I crave!"

*   *

"When a soul makes its life one of constant union with Mine I am greatly glorified and the soul gains much profit for others. Thus, a work in itself of little or no value, if steeped in My Blood or united to the labours I underwent during My mortal life, takes on such supernatural worth as to become of immense consequence for the saving of souls, results greater, perhaps, than if that soul had preached the gospel all over the world. . . . No matter if it be merely study, speech or writing . . . sewing, sweeping or only resting, so long as the action is prompted by obedience or by duty, and not done out of caprice. Then let it be done, too, in close union with Me, steeped in My Blood and with purity of intention.

"What I fain would have souls understand is that no action is of itself of importance; all that is worth considering is whether or no it is done in union with Me and with a pure intention.

"When, as a child, I swept and worked in the workshop of My foster father, I gave God as much glory as when I preached to crowds in My public life.

"There are many people who in the eyes of the world occupy important posts, and verily give great honour to My Heart. But I have a still greater number of humble workers who are very useful in My vineyard, for, acting out of pure love, they have learnt to overlay with supernatural gold the ordinary and common acts which they bathe in My Precious Blood.

"When they daily offer up their work to Me with the earnest desire that I should apply the merit thereof to souls—when they lovingly discharge their duties moment by moment, and hour by hour—how great is the treasure they amass in one day!

"To such souls I will discover My tender and inexhaustible love. It is so easy for the loving heart to let itself be guided by LOVE Itself."

* *

"WRITE, Josefa. I have more to tell thee for the souls I love! I wish them to know how absorbing is My desire for their perfection, which in substance consists in doing all ordinary and common actions in union with Me. If souls only grasped this principle, all their activities would be spiritualized. Who can reckon the value of one such divinized day?

"When a soul is aflame with longing to love, nothing comes amiss to her; but how hard and painful is the lot of the cold and spiritless. Let them, then, fly to My Heart to renew their flagging spirit . . . let them offer up their depression, uniting it to My burning zeal, then let them be assured that their every act will be of incomparable value to souls: My Heart well knows the depths of human frailty and is full of compassion for it.

"I do not want their union to Me to be of an indefinite character, but close and intimate, as that between those who live together in familiar friendship, and who, even when no word is spoken, yet have a constant regard and mutual attentions for one another —the result of their affection.

"When in consolation it is easy for a soul to think of Me, but when desolation and anguish replace it she must not fear—she need but cast a look on My Heart, which is so full of understanding, and this look will obtain from Me the most loving consideration.

"I will make her understand how much she is loved, in order that, in her turn, she may communicate to those I entrust to her ministrations what that love is of which she herself has had experience.

"My earnest desire is that all should constantly keep their eyes fixed on Me; let none descend to mediocrity, for this could only mean that they imperfectly understand the greatness of My affection for them.

"Oh, surely it is not hard to love Me, but easy and sweet; and to reach a high degree of friendship with Me nothing more is required in actions great or small than purity of intention and union with My Sacred Heart—all the rest will follow!

*   *

"My Heart is not only an abyss of love, but an abyss of mercy; and knowing, as I do, that even My closest friends are not exempt from human frailties, I intend that each of their actions, however insignificant, be clothed with immense value for the salvation of the world.

"All cannot preach or evangelize distant peoples, but there is none who cannot make My Heart known and loved. . . . By mutually helping one another they can prevent the loss of souls . . . because in My love and mercy I, too, will co-operate with them. Their generosity in sacrificing everything to Me releases an immense store of grace for the saving of sinners from the paths of sin.

"Souls I have specially chosen are given the mission of pouring out My graces over the world by love and sacrifice. The world is full of perils . . . countless souls are being led into sin, who need visible or invisible help. Alas! Again I remind My Own chosen emissaries that they deprive themselves and others of priceless treasures when they allow their daily opportunities to go to waste! Offer yours unworthy though they be— with the intention that all may come to a realization of the amazing mission which is theirs, by the fitting use of daily actions and efforts. Tell them that they are called to a high degree of intimacy with Me; how much I want them zealously to spread abroad that which will further My interests and glory. . . . Some know this well enough, but others do not fully realize it.

* *

"My love for them goes further still: not only shall I make use of their daily life by giving their least actions a divine value, but I will make use of their very failings and frailties, and even of their falls for the salvation of the world.

"When a soul sees clearly how wretched it is, it

ceases to attribute anything good to itself, and is forced to cloak itself in a certain measure of humility, which it would not possess were it less imperfect.

"Hence, when in the course of apostolic work or in the carrying out of its duties, a consciousness of their incapacity is forced upon them . . . or, when they experience a kind of repugnance to helping souls towards a perfection to which they know themselves to be still strangers, such helping souls are constrained to humble themselves in the dust. And should this self-knowledge impel them to My Feet, ashamed of their halting efforts, begging of My Heart the strength and courage they need, it is hardly possible for them to conceive how lovingly My Heart goes out to them and how marvellously fruitful I will make their labours.

"Those whose generosity is not equal to such strenuous endeavours and daily sacrifices will see their lives go by in perpetual resolutions which never come to fruition.

"But in this, distinguish: to souls that habitually promise and yet do no violence to themselves in order to prove their sincerity I say: 'Beware, lest all this straw and stubble should take fire or be scattered in an instant by the wind.' But there are others, and it is of them I now speak, who begin their day with a very good will and desire to prove their love by pledging themselves to self-denial or generosity in this or that circumstance, but when the time comes they are prevented by self-love, their temperament, health, or what not, from carrying out what a few hours before they quite sincerely purposed to do. Nevertheless, they speedily regain their self-mastery, acknowledge their instability of will, beg for pardon, then trustfully offer themselves once more to My Heart, renewing their resolution and repairing their fault by acts of generosity and love . . . these are the souls that greatly glorify Me and eventually perhaps do more good than if they had never fallen.*

"I want to be trusted; such faults of frailty I easily pardon, so long as I am loved! for they belong to human instability.

"But love transforms and divinizes all things, and there is no fault that mercy will not forgive. They are all swallowed up in its consuming fires!

"To forgive is My delight. Oh! to reign over hearts, and extend My peace to the extremities of the earth— what else do I desire? These are deeds worthy of love!

"I seek and shall find victims to repair for the sins of the world and obtain their forgiveness; I speak not of the many who, I know, long to please Me. Some generous souls there are who would give everything they have if only they were allowed to serve Me as I deem best for the accomplishment of My Will!

"Suffer and endure with Me, Josefa, that the world may know Me and come to Me. Suffering will triumph in love.

* *

"By the strength of love I will gain the victory over souls!

"I desire that they should be penetrated through

---

* Our Lord here establishes a very clear distinction between habitual venial sins, unresisted or consented to, and faults of fragility that are repaired.
He explains that the reparation gives Him more comfort than the fault of fragility displeases Him. In fact the humility, confidence and generosity implied in an act of reparation, presupposes awareness and complete consent of the will—a condition only partially fulfilled in the fault of fragility.

and through with true light, especially the innocent hearts of children who as yet know Me not and are growing up in cold indifference, ignorant of the value of their own souls. I want these new souls who are My especial delight, to find a shelter where they will be taught to know Me and where they may grow in the fear of My Law and the love of My Heart.

"You, Josefa, must be fuel to the fire I have come to cast upon the earth, for what is the use of lighting a fire if there is nothing to feed it with? That is why I want a chain of souls ablaze with ever-increasing love—the kind of love that trusts Me and depends entirely on Me—hearts kindled at *My* Heart, and ready in their turn to cast Its fire over all the earth!

*   *

"To-day I will speak to thee of My Cross, and of that only. By it I saved the world; by it I will bring the world back to the truths of Faith and to the Way of Love.

"To thee I will manifest My will: from the Cross I saved the world; that is to say that I did it through suffering.

Sin is an offence, against Infinite Majesty and calls for an infinite reparation; that is why I ask thee to offer up thy sufferings and labours, joined to the infinite merits of My Heart.

"Instil in the souls who come in contact with thee love and trust in the mercy of My Heart. And whenever thou canst speak of Me and make Me known, tell all souls to have no fear, because I am a God of love.

"Especially I recommend thee three things:

"1st. The practice of the Holy Hour, because it is one of the ways by which an infinite reparation can be offered up to God the Father through the mediation of Jesus Christ, His Divine Son.

"2nd. The devotion of the five Paters, in honour of My Wounds, since through them the world was saved.

"3rd. Constant union with the merits of My Divine Heart, because thou wilt thus give an infinite value to each of thy actions.

"Unceasingly have recourse to My Life, My Blood, My Heart . . . confide absolutely and without any fear in this Heart: It is a secret known to the few; I want thee to know it and to profit by it.

* *

"AND now lastly I address Myself to My Own consecrated ones, that they may make Me known to sinners and to the world.

"Many are as yet unable to understand what My true feelings are. They treat Me as One from Whom they live apart, know only slightly, and in whom they have little confidence. Let them rekindle their faith and love and live trustfully in My intimacy, loving and loved.

"It is usually the eldest son of the family who best knows the secrets and feelings of his father. In him the father is wont to confide more than in the younger ones, who as yet are unable to interest themselves in serious matters, or penetrate deeper than the surface. So when the father comes to die, it behoves the elder brother to transmit his wishes and will to these his younger brethren.

"In My Church I, too, have elder sons: they are those whom I Myself have chosen; consecrated by the priesthood or by the vows of religion. They are those who live nearest to Me; they share in My choicest graces, and to them I confide My secrets. Through their ministry they have charge of their brothers, My little children, and to them is entrusted either directly or indirectly the care of instructing and guiding them and of transmitting to them My Will.

"If these chosen souls truly know Me, they will be able to make Me known to others; if they love Me, they will be able to make Me loved; but how can they teach others when they hardly know Me themselves? Is there much love in one's heart for Him whom one does not know? Or what intimate converse is possible with One from whom association is cut off? What trust, where little confidence is felt?

"This is precisely what I wish to recall to the minds of My chosen ones; it is nothing new, no doubt, but have they no need to reanimate their faith, their love and trust?

"I want them to treat Me with greater intimacy—let them seek Me within their own hearts, for they know that a soul in a state of grace is the tabernacle of the Holy Spirit, and there let them consider Me as I truly am—their God, but a God of love. Let love triumph over fear, and, above all, let them never forget that I love them. Many are persuaded that it is because of this love that they were chosen, but when they are depressed at the sight of their wretchedness, then the thought may come to them that I have perhaps changed and love them less than formerly.

"How little such souls really know Me—how little they have understood what My Divine Heart is, for it is just their destitution and failings that incline My

Heart towards them, especially when in all humility they acknowledge their impotence and weakness, yet trustfully have recourse to Me—then, indeed, do they give Me more glory than before their fault.

"It is the same when they pray, either for themselves or for others; if they waver and doubt Me, it does not glorify My Heart.

"When the centurion came to beg Me to cure his servant, he said with great humility: 'I am not worthy that Thou shouldst enter under my roof,' . . . and he added—faith and trust prevailing—'Say but the word, and my servant shall be healed.' There was a man who interpreted my heart correctly—he knew I could not resist the supplications of one who trusted Me absolutely . . . He gave Me much glory thereby for to humility he joined confidence; yet I had made no manifestation to him as I have done to My chosen ones.

"Hope obtains innumerable graces, not only for oneself, but for others; this I wish thoroughly understood, so that My Heart may be revealed to those poor souls who as yet know Me not.

*　　*

"THERE are very few among the souls that are consecrated to Me that possess this unshakable confidence, because there are few who live in intimate union with Me.

"I would that all should know My wish, to see in them a renewal of the life of intimacy with Me; that they should not be satisfied with merely conversing with Me in church, where doubtless I am truly present, but remember that I abide in them, and delight in this incorporation.

"Let them speak to Me of all their concerns, consult Me at every turn . . . ask favours of Me. I live in them to be their life . . . I abide in them to be their strength . . . there I see them, hear them, love them. There I look for a return from them.

"Not a few are accustomed to a daily meditation; but for how many it becomes a mere formality, instead of a loving interview! They assist at Mass and receive Me in Holy Communion; on leaving the Church they become once more immersed in their own interests, so as to be totally oblivious of Me.

"A very desert is a heart to Me that neither speaks to Me nor asks anything of Me . . . and who, when in need of comfort, solicits it from creatures rather than ask it of her Creator who abides within her. Is this not a want of union, a lack of interior spirit—and to give its its true name, an absence of all love?

* *

"FURTHER, let Me once more tell those who are consecrated to Me how specially I selected and chose them, that they might live in union with Me, to comfort Me and repair for the sins of those who offend Me.

"Theirs is the duty of diligently contemplating My Heart, so as to share its emotions, and as far as in their power to realise its hopes.

"When a man works at his own field, how hard he toils at weeding out all noxious growths, sparing neither trouble nor fatigue till his object is attained. In like manner My chosen ones should set about the accomplishment of My wishes, so that as soon as they are known to them they should labour with zeal and ardour, undeterred by difficulty or suffering, that My glory may be increased and the sins of the world repaired.

"Write now, Josefa, for all consecrated souls, priests, religious men and women who are called by Me to a life of intimate union with Me.

"It is for them to know My longings and to share in My joys and sorrows.

"For them to labour at My interests, never sparing themselves trouble or pains.

"It is by prayer and penance that they will make reparation for many, many souls.

"It is for them, above all, to become more and more closely united to Me and never, never to abandon Me. Some forget that I look to them, My familiars, for consolation and companionship.

"And finally, it is for them to combine together, united in a bond of love in My Heart, to obtain truth, light and pardon for souls; and when they see with deep sorrow what outrages I receive, and feel impelled to offer themselves to make reparation by labouring in My vineyard, let them do so with unhesitating trust, for I could not refuse their petitions, and all they ask shall be granted them.

"Let all then apply themselves to the study of My Heart, striving to live in union with Me, to converse with Me and to consult Me. Let them unite their actions to My merits, bathe them in My Blood, and consecrate their lives to the saving of souls and the extension of My glory.

"Let them not descend to personal reflections which belittle them, but rejoice with expansion of heart at seeing themselves clothed with the authority of My

Blood and of My merits. If they rely on self they will do little or nothing, but if as My co-workers, they labour in My Name and for My glory, they will become all-powerful.

"Let these consecrated souls reawaken their wish to make reparation and beg confidently for the advent of the Divine King: that is, for My Universal Sovereignty.

"Let them hope and trust in Me, banishing all fear!

"Let them be consumed with zeal and charity for sinners . . . praying for them with compassionate hearts and treating them with all gentleness.

"Let all the world see in them My Goodness, My Love and My Mercy!

"Armed in their apostolic labours with prayer, penance and reliance on Me—never in themselves—let them go forward in the power and goodness of My Heart, which is ever with them.

"My apostles were poor and ignorant men, but rich and wise in the wealth and wisdom of God, and their watchword was: 'In Thy Name, O Lord, I shall labour and be all-powerful!'"

REPARATION

"I come, Belovèd, to seek My rest in thee . . . I am so little loved by men.

"I crave for love, and meet only with ingratitude! . . . How few are they that truly love Me.

"I ask thee to be ready every time I need thee to comfort My Heart. The solace of one faithful soul compensates for the poignant grief that comes to Me from the cold and indifferent.

"The anguish of My Heart thou wilt sometimes experience in thine and shalt thus alleviate My sorrow— fear not, for I am with thee!

"When I allow thee to feel cold, I do it in order to make use of thy ardour to quicken the souls of others. . . . "When I give thee over to the pangs of grief, thy pain deflects the Divine wrath which was about to strike the sinner. . . .

"When it seems to thee that thou art bereft of love, yet speakest words of endearment to Me, ah! then dost thou most of all comfort Me. . . .

"One single act of love coming from the depths of thy solitary heart repairs for the many acts of ingratitude committed against Me. Such acts do I lovingly reckon up—they are as precious as balm to Me.

"Thou must gain souls for Me, Josefa.

"In all thou dost, let love prevail.

"Let love alone be the motive of thy surrender, thy sufferings and thy labours.

99

"When I give thee comfort, accept it from Love's Hand.

"When I leave thee anguished and alone, accept it and suffer in love. I will make use of thee as a tired man makes use of a staff.

"It is My will to possess thee, enwrap thee, and to consume thee wholly.

*   *

"Listen to My words: 'Gold is purified in the fire'; so shall thy soul be strengthened and purified in tribulation, and thou shalt draw great profit for thyself and others out of the time of temptation.

"Enter deeply into My Heart, and there learn what zeal for God's Glory consumes It.

"Do not be afraid of suffering, if thereby thou canst in any way advance My Glory and save souls.

"How great is the value of a soul!

"Much suffering goes to the saving of one soul.

"Dost thou not know that I am inseparable from the Cross? If thou joinest thyself to Me, thou joinest thyself to the Cross; and when thou hast found the Cross, thou hast found Me.

"A true lover loves the Cross, and loving the Cross, loves Me; without love of the Cross and willing acceptance of it for love of Me none shall possess Eternal Life.

"The path of holiness and virtue is one of abnegation and suffering; the soul that generously embraces the Cross walks in true light; and she follows a straight and sure way, where she is in no danger of stumbling or falling.

"The Cross is a portal of true life, and every soul that

gladly embraces the Cross bestowed on her shall by its means enter into the splendours of Life Eternal.

"Dost thou now understand how precious is the Cross? Do not fear it . . . it comes from Me, and I will not suffer thee to lack strength to bear it.

"See how I, Myself, bore it for love of thee; do thou bear it for love of Me!

"Behold the Heart that from the Cross gave life to the world; in like manner My chosen ones must with complete submission stretch themselves on the Cross, following the example of their Saviour and their Master.

"The best reward I can give a soul is to single her out as a victim of Love and Mercy thus do I transform her into the likeness of Myself, who became a Victim for sinners.

"Wouldst thou know how best to comfort Me? Love Me, suffer for sinners and refuse Me nothing. Do not forget that I need souls to carry on the work of My Passion, that the wrath of God may be appeased. Nevertheless I Myself will help and succour thee.

* *

"When a sinner is prayed for by one who ardently desires his conversion, the petition will for the most part be granted, even if long deferred; My Heart finds in such prayer full reparation for the fault committed.

Prayer is never made in vain; for on the one hand it makes up for the injury inflicted by sin, and on the other obtains mercy, if not for that sinner, at all events for another who is better able to profit of the fruits of such a prayer.

"There are souls who in this life and for all Eternity

will give Me the glory which is due to Me from them, and over and above, that which some lost soul would have given Me. In this way My Glory remains undiminished, and one just man can repair the sins of many.

"My love for mankind is so great that it is as a martyrdom to Me when I see them wander from Me; not because of the glory they take from Me, but because of the unhappiness they are preparing for themselves.

"Souls are hurrying to perdition, yet for them I shed all My Blood, and in vain! But those who love Me and sacrifice themselves as victims of reparation attract the divine mercy; to these the world owes its salvation.

"Such souls are wanted to atone for all the offences committed against the Divine Majesty, and My Heart meanwhile is consumed with the desire to pardon!

"Poor sinners! How blind they are; I would so gladly forgive them, and they seek only to offend Me. . . . As Justice goes in pursuit of criminals, so do I pursue them, but Justice pursues to punish and I to pardon!

"The world casts itself headlong into enjoyment, and the multitude of sins committed overwhelms My Heart with bitterness and sorrow. Where shall I find alleviation to My sadness?

"Offer up thyself and thy whole person that My Justice may be appeased and the abuse of My Love atoned for. If thy own worthlessness is great, and thy sins without number, come and drown them all in the Blood that flows from My Heart, and be purified from thy stains. Then accept generously all the sufferings

I will send thee and offer them up to the Divine Majesty. Let your heart be fired with the hope of consoling an outraged God, and seize upon My merits wherewith to repair so many crimes.

"Tell Me: Is there anywhere a Heart more loving than Mine? Or one to whom so little response is made?

"And yet, in return, I receive only insults, . . .

"Poor souls! Let us go to implore for pardon and repair their sins: 'O My Father, have pity on them; do not chastise them according to their deserts, but forgive them. It is Thy Son that entreats Thee!'

*　　*

"I come to rest among My chosen ones. May they heal the wounds that I receive from sinners by their fidelity. Victims are needed to compensate Me for the afflictions with which My Heart is overwhelmed, and to ease the pain caused by so many faults.

"What malice! And how many men rush to perdition!

"The obstinacy of guilty souls is a deep wound to My Heart, but the loving tenderness of a faithful soul not only heals the wound, but is able to ward off the just anger of My Father.

"When, then, I send thee suffering, think not that I love thee less. It is because I need an antidote to the wounds of the world.

"I will take on Myself to make reparation for *thy* sins, but do thou repair for sinners.

"How vast is the number of those who sin against Me, and how many are lost eternally. Yet the direst wounds are inflicted on My Heart by those I dearly love and who are so sparing of themselves, never ready to sacrifice all. Yet do I not give them the whole of My Heart?

"Comfort Me, love Me, glorify Me through My Sacred Heart.

"Make satisfaction with It, and amends to the Divine Justice; offer it up as a victim of love for souls and very specially for those who are consecrated to Me.

"Live with Me, as I live with thee; hide thyself in Me, as I hide Myself in thee. We together will comfort each other, for when thou sufferest I also suffer, and My suffering shall be thine!

*   *

"Wilt thou console Me to-day? Ensconce thyself, then, deeply in My Heart. Present thyself to My Father, adorned with all the merits of thy Spouse. Beg pardon for so many ungrateful souls. Tell Him that thou, in spite of thy littleness, art ready to repair for the sins committed against Him.

"Tell Him how miserable a victim thou art, but cloaked in My Heart's Blood. Thus shalt thou spend the day, imploring forgiveness and making satisfaction.

"I wish thee to unite thy heart to the fire and zeal of Mine, that all may understand fully how I Myself shall be their joy and their reward.

"Let them not depart from My side . . . I love them so dearly!

*   *

"Behold the Wounds opened on the Cross to redeem mankind from eternal death and give them life. These wounds obtain mercy and pardon from My Father and will henceforth give sinners light and strength and love.

"This wound in My Heart shall be as an erupted volcano, at whose glowing fires souls shall be ignited. All the graces it contains are for them, that they may pour them out over the world, on those especially who know not where to seek them, and on others who despise them.

"I will shed My light on them that they may make use of this store-house of treasure, not only to make Me known and loved, but also to atone for sinners. Yes, the world is full of misdeeds, but it shall yet be saved by the expiation made by chosen souls.

"Love. For love is reparation, and reparation is love!"

LOVE

A love of intimacy with One Who is all LOVE, and Who, condescending to come down to the level of His Own creatures, asks them for their affection in return.

LOVE is all I ask! A docile love, that allows the Beloved to lead and guide it . . . a disinterested love, that seeks not its own enjoyment or its own interests, but those of the Beloved; a zealous love, burning and consuming, capable of overcoming every obstacle raised by selfishness: such is true love; it snatches the brand from the fire of Hell, where souls are hastening!

See My Heart . . . study it, and thou wilt learn from it how to love. True love is humble, generous and disengaged from self. If then thou desirest Me to teach thee how to love, begin by forgetting self. Let no sacrifice arrest thee, consider not the cost, ignore thy likes and dislikes: only love, and thou shalt have strength.

Many imagine that love consists in saying 'I love Thee, O my God,' but, sweet as love is, it yet is operative. This is the kind of love I wish thee to have; sweet and strong in labour and in rest, in prayer and consolation as in trouble and humiliation, ever giving proofs of love by deeds: in this true love consists.

If only this were well understood how quickly souls

would advance in perfection, and how much they
would console My Heart.

* *

TELL Me that thou lovest Me, this is a solace to my
aching Heart, for I hunger for thy love!

Would that I could see thee consumed with the
desire that others should love Me, and that thy Heart
should have no other sustenance.

Gaze upon My Heart and on the flames that consume It. These betoken My love for souls and especially for those consecrated to Me. For them I have a
special predilection . . . how few realize it.

But do thou enter into My Heart, taste its sweetness,
satiate thyself with its peace, and enkindle thine own
heart by contact with this heavenly flame.

Share My sorrow; in the long hours of My solitude
keep Me company. Love Me for the many who leave
Me forsaken and despised.

* *

LOVE makes all things easy. It yearns to suffer, for
suffering increases love. . . .

Love and suffering unite the soul intimately to God,
and make it one and the same thing with Him.

Many welcome Me when I visit them with consolation. They receive Me in Holy Communion with
great joy, but few open to Me, when I knock at their
door with the Cross.

When a soul is stretched on the Cross in complete
self-surrender then indeed it gives Me glory and is
very close to My Heart!

There are many it is true, who do not know Me, but
a far greater number knowing Me, have forsaken Me

to run after pleasure. How many are sensual! Who seek for nothing but enjoyment and are lost—for My way is a way of suffering and strewn with crosses. Love alone gives strength to enter on that path, hence My search for those who love.

When two friends love one another, a very small breach of consideration in one of them is sufficient to wound the other. And so it is with My Heart. I would like those who aspire to intimacy with Me to refuse Me nothing. If I find in thee sympathy and consideration, never will I let Myself be outdone by thee in generosity. I shall flood thy soul with peace, nor ever leave thee desolate—for thy littleness shall be changed into greatness, for it is I Myself that live in thee!

* *

My heart is unable to contain Itself, so great is its desire to bestow Itself, to yield Itself, to dwell always with Its creatures. Oh! How I long for them to open their hearts to Me, to enclose Me in theirs, that the fire which consumes Mine may strengthen and enkindle theirs. Then shall I become all in all to them—I shall be their Father if they lack a father; their Spouse if they desire Me as such; I will be their vigour if they are without strength—and should they desire to comfort Me I shall let them do so.

My one wish is to make the gift of Myself to them, and to pour out on them all the graces I have prepared for them.

* *

Let Me rejoice in thee; My greatness will replace thy lowliness; we shall labour together, I living in thee and thou spending thyself for souls. My Heart will do all that is necessary—Mercy will come into play and Love will annihilate thy whole being. The less there is of thyself, the more I shall become thy life, and thou shalt be to Me a heaven of rest!

Speak to Me, for I am with thee; thou art not alone because thou seest Me not, I am there and I hear thee. Speak to Me, smile at Me, for I am thy inseparable companion.

It is thy very littleness that pleases Me, and I ask only two things of thee: love and surrender; be as an empty vessel, and I will fill it: on thy part have no measure in love; just love, and leave it to thy Maker to have care of thee, who art the work of His Hands.

If thou art poor, I am rich—if thou art weak, I am strength itself; do not refuse Me anything whatsoever. I will be thy defender and raise thee up; if thou leave thyself in My Hands I will do all.

* *

My will is that all that thou dost should be offered to Me, even thy smallest actions; to compensate My Heart for the sufferings inflicted by those especially who are consecrated to Me.

Repose without fear in My Heart. By gazing upon It thou wilt see to how great an extent It is able to put an end to all that is still imperfect in thee.

Surrender thyself into My Hands, and have no other care than that of pleasing Me. Think of Me as thy Father, thy Saviour and thy God. My Heart is an abyss of love, make thy way into It and fear not.

Do I ask thee to merit the graces I bestow on thee?

No, only to accept them from Me; leave Me a free hand in thee.

Mine Eyes are riveted on thee, do thou fix thine on Me.

I make little account of thy nothingness, even of thy faults, for everything is wiped out in My Blood—it is enough for thee to know that I love thee. Commit thyself into My Hands.

*   *

WHEN a soul in truth surrenders all things to Me, so great is My contentment, that notwithstanding her faults and imperfections, I take My delight in her, and abide complacently within her.

If thou dost give up all else for Me, in My Heart thou shalt find it again.

I need loving hearts! Souls who atone for sin. . . . Above all souls that have surrendered all to Me!

My Eyes are open wide to lead and guide thee, so let thyself go blindfolded and trusting.

When thou callest Me thy Father, I cast on thee a look of complacency, and My Heart is concerned to take care of thee. When a little one begins to babble, and utters for the first time the sweet name of 'Father,' tender parents press their child with transports to their hearts, knowing no greater pleasure in the world! How much more than an earthly father and mother am I to thee, Father, Mother, God, Creator, Saviour, Spouse! And One whose love is unequalled!

Yea, Beloved—when thou art oppressed and in anguish, come hasten to call on thy Father, and find thy rest in His Heart.

If in the midst of thy work thou canst not cast thyself at My Feet . . . only whisper this one word 'Father' and I will help thee, guide and comfort thee.

* *

BEHOLD this Heart! It is the OPEN BOOK wherein to meditate. It will teach thee all virtues, especially zeal for My Glory and the salvation of souls.

Look well and long on this Heart: It is the SANCTUARY of the afflicted, hence, thine, for where find one more miserable than thou?

Gaze into My Heart—it is the CRUCIBLE in which the most defiled are purified, and afterwards inflamed with love; come, draw near this furnace, cast in it thy faults and sins; have confidence and believe in Me who am thy Saviour.

Once more fix thine eyes intently on My Heart: It is a FOUNTAIN of living water: throw thyself into Its depths and appease thy thirst. Oh! that all should come and find refreshment at this source.

As for thee! I have found a hidden place for thee in the mystery of My Heart . . . thou art so feeble that alone thou couldst not attain to it . . . use well the graces there stored for thee . . . let My love have free play in thee and remain always lowly.

Thou sayest well 'Thou art good'; really to comprehend it, souls need only union with Me and interior life.

If they lived more united to Me, how much better they would know Me! To effect this must be our joint work, from Heaven we shall teach them how to live united to Me, in closest intimacy, and not as with one who is far off. Do I not live in them by grace?

If My Chosen Ones lived thus, what an amount of

good they could do to poor souls who are far from Me, and know Me not.

Once their union with Me has been effected, then they will know how many sins are committed against Me, and they will be able better to understand My feelings and they will console Me and atone for sinners . . . then, too, full of trust in My goodness, they will ask and obtain pardon for the world.   Thou lovest Me because I am good, in return I love thee because thou art lowly, and this lowliness is dedicated to Me.

CONFIDENCE

That is: Security in Him Who is goodness and mercy, and Who gives a special call to souls, that living with Him and knowing Him, they may look to Him for everything.

I AM He who forgives thee thy sins, who wipes out thy offences, and who sustains thy weakness!

The greater is thy nothingness, the more My power upholds thee: I will enrich thee with My gifts, and if thou art faithful I will take sanctuary in thy heart and fly to it when sinners repudiate Me. I will rest in thee, and thou shalt have life in Me.

If thou art an abyss of wretchedness, I am an abyss of sweetness and of mercy. My Heart is thy refuge, come, there to seek all thou hast need of; even such things as I require at thy hands.

Instead of looking at thy nullity, look at the power of My Heart that upholds thee and have no fear. I am thy strength and shall heal thy wounds.

What canst thou fear from Me? Never question My love for thee, or the clemency of My Heart. Thy misery draws Me to thee . . . without Me what art thou? Never forget that I am all the closer to thee, in proportion to thy lowliness.

Nor grieve overmuch at thy falls—cannot I make a Saint of thee? I will seek thee out in thy nothingness to unite Myself to thee, only never refuse Me anything.

The void and misery in thee are as magnets that

attract My love to thee. Yield not to discouragement, for My Mercy is honoured in thy infirmity.

It is a comfort to My Heart to be able to forgive; what greater joy or wish have I than that?

When after a fall a soul returns to Me, she gains by having thus consoled Me, for I cast on her a glance of love. What do her shortcomings signify to Me provided her one and only desire is to glorify Me. Such a lowly soul obtains grace for many others.

Would that thou couldst understand to what lengths I would go in pardoning faults of pure fragility. Be not troubled at them, for thy very frailty attracts Me.

* *

GLADLY would I enshrine thee in My Heart, for love knows no measure and in spite of failings and transgressions on thy part, I will use thee to make others know that I am merciful and that I love them.

There are too many who still do not realise the goodness of My Heart, if they would but cast themselves headlong into that bottomless abyss and lose themselves therein for ever!

I am thy SAVIOUR, I am thy SPOUSE! Words too little understood. . . . That work I wish to do through thee. My great aim is to save sinners, and I want those consecrated to Me to understand how easily they can win souls. I will make them conscious what treasures they allow to escape them, by not meditating sufficiently on these two words: SAVIOUR and SPOUSE.

My Heart is drawn to thee and I am not repelled by thy lowliness; nay, just because of it, with divine folly do I love thee.

I am the Sun of Justice, and in its splendour thou perceivest thy worthlessness; the greater it is, the more should the tenderness of thy love increase.

If thy soul is a fruitless soil, incapable of producing anything, I am the husbandman that tills it, that sends forth warm rays of the sun to purify it, then . . . My Hand shall scatter seed.

* *

My Cross rests on thy abjectness, and I repose in thy humility. My Cross shall strengthen and support thee. Grasp it fearlessly, for I will not allow it to exceed thy strength; have I not reckoned up thy stature, and weighed thee in the balance of My love?

The smaller a thing is the easier it is to handle; therefore is it that I can use thee according to My good pleasure.

Never think that thy sinfulness will make Me love thee less—no, My Heart loves thee and will never abandon thee. Thou knowest that fire burns and destroys, but the attributes of My Heart are pardon, purification and love. Do I not know thy weakness and thy faults?—but the flames of My Heart will purify and consume them all.

How often have I told thee that I will and desire that souls should give Me their imperfections; I say to thee: if thou darest not approach Me, I Myself will come to thee.

The greater thy weakness, the greater shall be My

affection for thee. Let go all thy imperfections, am I not their Lord and Master?

Thy humility leaves room for My greatness, thy misery and sins for My mercy . . . thy trust for My fondness and pity. Come! Lean upon this Heart, and take thy rest.

*   *

WHEN a King espouses the daughter of a subject, he assumes the obligation of providing all that the new rank to which he has raised her requires.

I have chosen you and have undertaken to provide for your every want. I require nothing of you beyond that which you already have. Give Me an empty heart and I will fill it, give it to Me destitute of all adornment, and I will embellish it. Give it to Me with all its sordidness and I will consume it. That which is hidden from you, I will reveal, and all that you lack I take on Myself to supply.

*   *

THERE are a great number of souls who believe in Me, but few who believe in My love, and among those who believe in My love there are few who trust in My tenderness and pity. Many acknowledge Me for their God, but few look on Me as their Father.

But I shall manifest Myself and make it clear to souls that I ask nothing of them that they do not already possess. What I do demand is complete surrender on their part, for all they have belongs to Me.

If they possess only wretchedness and nothingness, or even only faults and sins, let them offer these. Give them to Me, give them all to Me, and let them only retain perfect trust in My Heart. I forgive you all, I love you all, and will Myself sanctify you.

PART III

THE PASSION OF OUR LORD
JESUS CHRIST

CONTEMPLATIONS:

February 22nd, 1923.

JESUS WASHES THE FEET OF HIS DISCIPLES

I WILL begin by discovering to thee the thoughts that filled My Heart while washing the feet of My apostles.

Mark how the whole Twelve were gathered together —none excepted: John the Beloved was there, and Judas, who was so soon to deliver Me to My enemies.

I will tell thee why I willed to have them all assembled together and why I washed their feet.

*   *

I GATHERED them all together because the moment had come for My Church to be manifested to the world, and for all the sheep to have but one Shepherd.

It was My intention to show that I never refuse grace, even to those who are guilty of grave sin; nor do I exclude them from the company of the good, whom I love with predilection. I keep them all in My Heart, that each may receive the help required by their state of soul.

Sadly did I see in the person of My unhappy disciple Judas the throng of those who gathered at My feet, washed with My Blood, would yet be hastening to their eternal perdition.

To these I would give to understand that it is not the fact of being in sin that ought to keep them from Me—they must never think that there is no remedy for them, or that they have forfeited for ever the love that once was theirs. . . . No, poor pitiable souls! The God who has shed all His Blood for you has no such feelings towards you!

Come to Me and fear not, for I love you all! I will wash you in My Blood and you shall be made whiter than snow; all your offences submerged in the waters of mercy, nor shall anything whatsoever be able to tear from My Heart its love for you!

* * *

Josefa, let an ardent desire to see all these souls come to penance seize hold of thee! Confidence, not fear, should animate them, for I am a God of Pity, ever ready to open My Heart that they may take refuge therein.

THE LAST SUPPER

COME, My confidante, and listen to more of Love's secrets: I will tell thee to-day of My reasons for washing the feet of My disciples before the Last Supper.

*   *

IT was to teach souls in the first place how pure they must be to receive Me in Holy Communion.

It also signified for the Sacrament of Penance, by which those who have had the misfortune to sin recover their innocence.

And I did it with My own Hands, in order that those who have consecrated themselves to apostolic labours may follow My example, and treat sinners with humility and gentleness, as also all others that are entrusted to their care. I girded Myself with a white linen cloth to remind them that apostles need to be girded with abnegation and mortification, if they hope to exert any real influence on souls. . . .

I wished also to teach them that mutual charity, which is ever ready to excuse the faults of others, to conceal them and to extenuate them, and never to reveal them.

Lastly, the water poured on the feet of My apostles denoted the zeal which burned in My Heart for the salvation of the world.

*   *

THE hour of Redemption was at hand. My heart could no longer restrain Its love for mankind or bear the thought of leaving them orphans.

So, to prove My tenderness for them and in order to remain always with them till time has ceased to be, I resolved to become their food, their support, their life, their all.

Could I but make known to all the loving sentiments with which My Heart overflowed at My Last Supper, when I instituted the Sacrament of the Holy Eucharist. . . .

My glance ranged across the ages, and I saw the multitudes who would subsist on My Body and Blood, and all the good it would effect. I saw the hearts that from Its contact would bud forth virginity, and the thousands it would awaken to deeds of charity and zeal—how many martyrs of love would cluster round Me in serried ranks, how many who had been enfeebled by sin and the violence of passion would come back to their allegiance and recover their spiritual energy by partaking of this bread of the strong!

Who can describe the overwhelming feelings that filled My soul—of joy, of love, of tenderness, and alas, of bitter sadness?

*   *

LATER we shall continue, Josefa. Go now in My peace; console Me, and do not be afraid; the well-spring of My Blood is not exhausted, and It will cleanse thy soul.

March 2nd, 1923.

THE BLESSED SACRAMENT AND SINNERS

YEA, I must tell, too, of the poignant sorrows of the
Last Supper! If it was bliss to Me to think of all those
to whom I should be both Companion and Heavenly
Food, of all who would surround Me to the end of
time with adoration, reparation and love, it in no wise
diminished My grief at the many who would leave
Me deserted in My Tabernacle and who would dis-
believe in My Real Presence.

I would have to enter into hearts defiled by sin—
forced to enter; and how often this profanation of My
Body and Blood would serve for their ultimate condemnation.

Sacrileges and outrages, and all the nameless
abominations to be committed against Me passed
before My eyes . . . the long lonely hours of the day
and of the night in which I would remain forsaken and
alone on the altars, and the multitudes who would
listen unheeding to the appeals of My Heart.

Am I not a Prisoner of Love in the Blessed Sacrament; do I not stay there that all may come and find
the comfort they need; the tenderest of Hearts, the
best of Fathers, the most faithful of Friends?

Yet how few are they who make any return for a
love that exhausts and consumes Itself for them.

That I may be Life to sinners, I live in their midst;

and that I may be their Physician and the remedy of the diseases bred by corrupt nature; and in return they forsake Me, insult and despise Me! . . .

Poor, pitiable sinners! . . . Ah, come to Me; day and night I am on the watch for your approach; nor will I cast your sins in your face, but wash them in My Blood and in My Wounds. No need to be afraid if only you will come—you know how dearly you are loved! . . .

And you, dear souls, why this coldness and indifference on your part? Do I not know that family cares, household concerns and the requirements of your position in life make continual calls on you? But cannot you spare a few minutes in which to prove your affection and your gratitude? Too easily you allow yourselves to be involved in useless and incessant cares. Will you not for love of a prisoner spare a few moments to visit Him?

"Were you weak or ill, surely you would find time to see a doctor? Come, then, to One who is able to give both strength and health to your soul, and bestow the alms of love on the Divine Mendicant who watches for you, calls for you and longs to see you at His side.

March 6th, 1923.

THE HOLY EUCHARIST AND CONSECRATED SOULS

I AM about to reveal My Mystery of Love to thee, Josefa, for those souls who are chosen and consecrated.

When about to institute the Holy Eucharist, I saw

the privileged throng who would be nourished by My Body and Blood, and find in It the remedy for their shortcomings, a consuming fire for their imperfections with which to inflame their love.

I likewise saw them gathered round Me as in a garden closed, and each separately rejoicing Me with her flowers and perfume. As a vivifying Sun, My Sacred Body gave them life, and warmed up their cold hearts. To some I went for comfort, to others as a refuge; to others again for rest. . . . Would that all these cherished souls knew how easily they can console Me, harbour Me or give Me rest—to Me who am their God!

It is this infinitely loving God who has given you your vocation and has mysteriously attracted you into the enclosed Garden of His delight: the God who is your Saviour has made Himself your Spouse!

And He Himself feeds you with His Immaculate Flesh and slakes your thirst with His Blood, and will be for evermore your rest and your joy.

* *

ALAS, why is it that so many who have been endowed with My choicest graces now become a cause of pain to My Sacred Heart? Am I not always the same? Have I changed? No, My love is unalterable and will endure to the end of time, with the same tenderness and preference.

That you are unworthy, I well know; but not for that do I turn away from you. On the contrary, with anxious solicitude I look for your coming, that I may not only ease your troubles, but also grant you many favours.

If I ask for your love, do not refuse it; it is so easy to love Love Itself.

If I should ask you for things that cost, know that My grace will never be wanting nor the strength you need to conquer yourself.

I hope to find in you My comfort, therefore have I chosen you. Open your whole soul to Me, and if you are conscious of its defects, say with humility and trust: "Lord, Thou who knowest both the flowers and the fruits of my garden, come, and teach me how I may grow that which will please Thee most."

To one who holds this language and has a genuine desire of showing love I answer: "Belovèd, if such is thy desire, suffer *Me* to grow them for thee; let Me delve and dig in thy garden; let Me clear the ground of those sinewy roots that obstruct it and which thou hast not the strength to pull up. Maybe I shall ask thee to give up certain fads, or curb thy temper . . . do some act of charity, or of patience, or self-denial—or perhaps prove thy love by zeal, obedience or abnegation; all such deeds help to fertilize the soil of thy soul, which then can produce the flowers and fruit I look for. . . . Dost thou know what I most hope to find? That by thy self-conquest some sinner has obtained light; that thy ready patience under provocation has healed the wounds he had inflicted on Me; repaired for his offences and expiated his faults . . . a reproof accepted with joy and no sign of impatience, obtained for a sinner blinded by pride, the courage to humble himself.

All this I will do for thee, if thou wilt give Me the chance. Then not only will blossoms expand in thy soul, but thou wilt be to Me the consolation that My Heart craves for.

"Lord, Thou knowest my readiness to let Thee do with me whatsoever Thou willest. . . . Alas! I have fallen and displeased Thee. . . . Canst Thou forgive me once again? I am so wretched and can do no good!"

Yes, My Belovèd, and I am comforted, for if thou hadst not fallen perchance thou hadst never made this act of humility and love.

All this was present to Me when I instituted the Blessed Sacrament, and My Heart glowed with the desire of becoming Food for just such souls; for if I take up My abode among men, it is not merely to live among the perfect, but to uphold the weak, to sustain the lowly. I Myself will cause them to grow and become strong—in their indigence I will rest, and their good resolves will be My solace.

* * *

But there are some among these chosen souls who will inflict sorrow on Me—for will they all persevere? Such is the cry of grief that breaks from My Heart—a lamentation which should reach them.

* * *

Enough for to-day, Josefa, farewell! You comfort Me when you trust yourself entirely into My Hands. . . . I cannot every day speak to souls, so let Me tell thee My secrets for them—and make use of thee whilst thou art still in this life.

THE HOLY EUCHARIST SLIGHTED, ASTONISHING MARVEL OF LOVE

Write to-day concerning the pain endured by My Heart, when being constrained by the fire that consumed It, I devised the marvel of love that the Holy Eucharist is. And while My glance roamed over those many souls that would feed on this heavenly Bread, I could not but see also the indifference by which so many others . . . consecrated souls and souls of priests would wound and hurt Me in this Sacrament. There were those who would gradually yield to routine, weariness, and lassitude, to end perhaps in tepidity.

* *

Still, I wait and watch in the Tabernacle for that soul, fervently hoping that she will come, that she will converse with Me with all the unconstrained sincerity of a Spouse, asking My advice and begging for My grace.

"Come," I say to her, "let us discuss everything with perfect freedom . . . be concerned about sinners . . . offer thyself to make reparation for them . . . promise Me that at least to-day thou wilt not leave Me forsaken; then reflect and see if My Heart is not asking something more of thee to comfort It."

So much do I hope to obtain from that soul and of many another. Yet when she receives Me in Holy Communion she barely adverts to My Presence; she is hurrying on to something else, or she is tired and put out . . . her whole mind is absorbed by her occupations, her family cares, or maybe by anxiety for her health; she is indifferent, bored, wishes it were time to go! Is it thus that thou receivest Me, O soul for whom I have watched with all the impatience of love throughout the livelong night?

Yes, I yearned for her coming that I might share her anxieties . . . and bestow on her the fresh graces prepared for her . . . but she does not care or want them, she has nothing to ask Me, and just murmurs without so much as addressing Me! Why, then, has she come? Was it simply out of routine, to go through a customary formality, or perhaps only because no grave sin prevented it? Neither love nor a wish for close union with Me impelled her coming. Alas, what a disappointment of the delicate feelings I had hoped to find in her.

* *

And priests? Who can express all I expect from the priesthood. They are invested with My own power, that they may forgive sin. I Myself am obedient to their word when they summon Me from Heaven to earth. . . . I am totally surrendered into their hands; they may confine Me to the Tabernacle or give Me to the faithful in Holy Communion.

To each I have entrusted souls that they may by their example guide them in the path of truth and perfection.

I—o

What response do they make? Are there none who are oblivious of Love's mission?

Will this My minister at the altar have something to tell Me about his charges to-day? Will he make reparation to Me for the offences, the secret of which has been entrusted to him? Will he entreat of Me the graces he needs to carry on his sacred ministry? Zeal for souls, courage in self-sacrifice, more to-day than yesterday? Will all his affection be wholly Mine, and shall I be able entirely to rely on him as on a trusty and well-beloved disciple?

Oh, how cruelly My Heart is riven, when I have to say: "The world wounds Me in My Hands and in My Feet, and it sullies My Countenance. . . . My Chosen and set-apart, religious . . . priests . . . *they* rend and break *My Heart!*

Now thou knowest what anguish oppressed Me at the Last Supper when I saw Judas in the midst of the Twelve . . . the very first traitor among the apostles . . . and after him . . . so many more, so many more, in the course of ages!

*   *

The Blessed Sacrament is a device prompted by love. It is Life and Fortitude of souls, a remedy for all faults, and Viaticum for the last passage from time to eternity.

In It sinners recover peace; tepid souls, the warmth that gives them new life; pure souls find in It sweet honey and rarest sustenance; fervent souls tranquillity and the satisfaction of every longing; saintly souls, wings to fly towards perfection.

Consecrated souls find in It a dwelling, deep affection, and Life. Therein they shall seek and find a perfect exemplar of those sacred and hallowed bonds that intimately and inseparably unite them to their heavenly Bridegroom.

March 12th, 1923.

GETHSEMANE

COME with Me, Josefa, to Gethsemane, and let thy soul sink into heaviness and sorrow with Mine.

After having preached to great crowds, healed the sick, given sight to the blind, raised the dead . . . after having lived three years with My apostles to teach them and entrust My doctrine to them . . . I finally willed to teach them fraternal love by example, and how mutually to serve each other; and this I did by washing their feet and making Myself their food.

"The hour had come for the Son of God made Man, Redeemer of the human race, to shed His Blood and give His Life for the world. And that I might surrender Myself to My Father's Will I forthwith betook Myself to prayer.

*   *

DEARLY loved souls, come, listen to My voice: The one thing necessary is surrender to God's Will in humble submission, the rebellion of nature notwithstanding.

Add yet another; that all important actions should, following My example, be preceded and vivified by prayer, for only in prayer can a soul obtain the strength needed in life's difficulties. In prayer God will manifest Himself, will counsel and inspire, even if His action be unfelt.

I retired into the Garden of Gethsemane—that is to say, into solitude. God is to be sought within, away from distraction and noise. Silence is the atmosphere wherein nature is conquered by grace. Interior arguments prompted by self-love or sensuality are obstacles to union with God.

In order to give you an example, My beloved ones, I took with Me three of My disciples—from which learn that the three Powers of your soul must accompany and help you in your prayer.

Let MEMORY recall the benefits and perfections of your God—His power, goodness, love and mercy. Let your UNDERSTANDING seek out ways of responding to the manifold marvels with which He has surrounded you. Let the WILL be strengthened in its resolve to do ever more and better for Him. Offer yourselves to work for sinners in apostolic labours, or in the silence and retirement of a humble and laborious office. Adore profoundly as it beseems a creature before the Creator, and while you accept all His designs in your regard, submit yourselves entirely to His Will.

It was thus I offered Myself to carry out the Redemption of the world.

How terrible was the hour in which I felt all the torments of My Passion burst overwhelmingly upon Me . . . the calumnies, the insults, the scourging, the thirst, the Cross! All these thronged before My eyes and pressed in upon My Heart! At one and the same time I saw all the offences, sins and crimes that were to be committed throughout the ages—I witnessed them all, and was invested in them, so that under the burden of their ignominy I was constrained to present Myself before the Face of the All-Holy and implore Him to show Mercy!

And there burst upon Me the wrath of an angry and offended God, and in order to appease His Majesty I offered Myself as security for sinful man.

But so great was the anguish, so mortal the agony of My human nature under the strain and weight of so much guilt, that a bloody sweat poured from Me to the ground.

O sinners, who thus torture Me, will this Blood be for your condemnation or your salvation? Can it be that this sweat, this anguish, this agony shall be for many all in vain?

It is enough for to-day, Josefa—remain close to Me in Gethsemane, that My Blood may fertilize and strengthen the root of thy littleness.

JESUS FINDS HIS APOSTLES ASLEEP

Josefa, let us continue in prayer: stay near Me, and when thou seest Me submerged in an ocean of grief, rise, and with Me go to the three disciples I had left a stone's-throw away.

I had chosen them that they might share in My agony, pray with Me and by their company afford Me some consolation. . . . What thinkest thou were My feelings to find them asleep? O the pang of loneliness, and to have none to share in My sorrow!

How often My suffering Heart hopes to find solace among the souls It loves, and how often It finds them slumbering! . . .

If I attempt to awaken them, to make them come out of themselves and their preoccupations, the reply that reaches Me in acts if not in words amounts to: "I cannot now, I am too busy . . . too tired, the effort is too great . . . I need repose." Then gently insisting, I say to this soul: "Do not be afraid to sacrifice thyself for Me. Cannot I reward thee? Come for a little while . . . only for one hour. . . . I need thee. Come, pray with Me, before it is too late." And the same answer is repeated. . . .

Poor soul, canst thou not watch one hour with Me? Soon, maybe, I will return . . . but no longer shalt thou hear Me, for thou wilt be deaf in sleep! If I offer thee grace, of what use to one so drowsy and somnolent? Is there any hope that later on thou wilt be roused? Is there not danger that one so soul-starved will be too weak to rise from its torpor?

How many have been surprised by death in the midst of their slumbers . . . alas! think of their awakening.

Beloved souls, learn from this how useless it is to seek comfort in creatures. They are oftenest heavy and sluggish, and their indifference increases our distress at finding no response to our affectionate expectations.

* *

I WENT back to My prayer, and falling on My Face, I worshipped My Father and implored His help. I did not call Him "My God," but "My Father." It is when harrowed by pain that you, too, must call on your Father; beg for His help, expose your woes and fears, and let your cry of anguish remind Him that you are His Child. Tell Him how exhausted you are . . . that your soul is experiencing what seems a very sweat of blood. Pray confidently and expect relief from your Father's heart. Doubt not that He will Himself comfort you, whether what you suffer is from personal causes or from anxiety for the souls under your care. You will be strengthened to go through with it.

My soul, already shattered and a prey to sadness, had still to endure deadly anguish, crushed by the weight of the blackest ingratitude; for notwithstanding the Blood now pouring from My Body and which I was shortly to shed from countless Wounds, innumerable souls would be lost . . . a still greater number would sin against Me, and myriads would not so much as have heard of My Name . . . yet this did not deter Me from sacrificing My Life for each in particular, and seeking to benefit each by My merits. . . . Blood of a God! Infinite merits! Yet to be in vain for how great a number!

This is the Chalice I accepted and drank to the dregs.

I did it, O souls that I love, to teach you not to faint under your burdens. Never count them as useless, even if you are unable to reckon the result; the day will come when you will reap the benefit of every pang—but for now, submit yourself to the divine Will, leaving It free to do with you whatsoever It wills.

*   *

March 14th, 1923.

THE TREASON OF JUDAS

After having been comforted by an Angel sent by My Father, I saw Judas coming, one of the Twelve, and with him those who had come to take Me prisoner. They carried ropes, staves and stones to seize and bind Me. I arose, and drawing near, I said to them: "Whom seek ye?" Then Judas, embracing Me, gave Me a kiss. Ah, Judas, what art thou about to do? Why this kiss?

*   *

To how many souls can I not also say: "What are you doing? . . . Why do you betray Me with a kiss?"

O soul that art so loved by Me, how is it that thou comest to receive Me, to assure Me of thy affection,

and hardly hast thou left Me than already thou hast
betrayed Me to My enemies? Thou knowest right
well that in that company which so attracts thee,
stones will be cast at Me, by which I mean those
conversations that wound Me—and thou who hast
communicated this morning wilt do so again to-morrow.
These are the occasions in which My costly grace is
imperilled.

And how about transactions of doubtful integrity?
Such as would make it unlawful for thee to acquire
certain gains, to obtain maybe a rise in social position,
to secure thee greater comfort. In so doing thou fol-
lowest the example of Judas: with a kiss thou greetest
Me, and in a few moments, a few hours at most, thou
wilt give My enemies a sign that, recognizing Me,
they may lay hands on Me.

"Not only dost thou bind My hands, but thou
castest stones at Me by that friendship that fetters thee
and causes another to bind and stone Me likewise.

Why dost thou betray Me thus, thou who knowest
Me and so often hast gloried in thy almsgiving and
church-going? . . . These acts which might be highly
meritorious are actually a "cloak of thy malice." O
soul whom I love, why art thou enslaved by passion?
I do not ask thee to free thyself, for I well know that
it is not in thy power, but I do ask thee to keep up the
struggle against thy passions. Ephemeral pleasure is
the price for which Judas sold Me—and what did he
gain? The loss of his soul!

How many have sold and will sell Me for a passing
pleasure, the enjoyment of a moment. . . . Alas, poor
souls, whom seek ye? Is it I? This Jesus whom you

knew and loved, and whom once you were under obligation to love solely and only, for ever and ever!

Listen to My words: "Watch and pray, fight your evil inclinations and suffer them not to grow into confirmed habits."

The grass in meadowlands has to be mown year by year, and in some cases even at every recurring season. The ground needs to be ploughed up, manured and freed from weeds. And so must souls be worked at and evil tendencies carefully corrected.

Do not imagine that one who betrays Me is led to do so by one grave sin. Though it is possible, the case is rare—the greatest falls are the result of neglect of little things—a small satisfaction indulged, a moment of weakness yielded to, a consent to do a thing in itself lawful but immortified—a pleasure, not sinful, but ill-advised for you here and now. All these little things recur unheeded, and little by little the soul is blinded, grace loses its power, passion increases and finally triumphs.

Oh, how infinitely sorrowful for the Heart of God, whose love is boundless, to see so many insensibly approaching nearer and nearer the abyss.

March 15th, 1923.

THE PETTY BETRAYALS OF HIGHLY-GIFTED SOULS

I have told thee, Josefa, how those who offend Me gravely become My enemies; the arms they use against Me are their sins.

I wish to-day to explain to thee that it is not a question of major lapses. There are souls, and even highly-favoured ones, that are false to Me, by habitual imperfections, by evil tendencies acquiesced in, concessions to immortified nature, and failings against charity. . . . If sin and ingratitude are hard for My Heart to bear, how much more grievous to endure them from those whom I dearly love!

Others, however, can comfort and console Me.

O Chosen Souls, whom I have marked out for My Home of Rest, the Garden of My delights, I do indeed expect more from you—tenderness, considerate attentions prompted by love!

You can be to Me a healing balm for My grievous Wounds; you can cleanse My scarred and defiled countenance; you can help Me to enlighten blind souls who in the darkness of night prey upon Me to bind and lead Me to death.

Leave Me not alone! Awake, let us go, behold the enemy is at hand!

* *

WHEN the soldiers came forward to seize Me, I said
to them: "It is I." Such, too, is the word I utter when
a soul is about to yield to temptation: "It is I." Yes,
"It is I." It is not too late; I am ready to forgive, if
thou willest it. Then it shall not be thou that bindest
Me with chains of sin, but I that shall bind thee with
chains of love! Come; I am He who loves thee, who
pities thy weakness and longs to open My arms and
gather thee to My Heart's embrace.

Alas! how sick at heart I am when, after words so
tender, there still remain some who would bind and
lead Me to My death!

* *

THE hour of sacrifice had struck and its accomplishment was at hand, so yielding to the soldiery, I gave
Myself up into their hands and was led as a lamb to the
slaughter!

They dragged Me to the house of Caiphas, where
they heaped on Me insults and mockery, and where
one of the soldiers struck Me a blow in the face.

The first buffet! . . . mark My words Josefa: did it,
think you, give Me more pain than the scourges of
the flagellation? . . . No, but I saw in this first blow
the first mortal sin of many souls who had lived till
then in My grace . . .—a first mortal sin! Opening
the door to so many more, and how great the number
who would follow that example, and fall into the same
danger . . . perhaps into a like misfortune, and so on
to death in mortal sin!

* *

TO-MORROW we shall continue; meanwhile, Josefa,
spend the day in prayer, that light may be given to
those following this dangerous path.

THE DENIAL OF PETER

Continue writing for the sake of souls.

My disciples have all fled; Peter, impelled by curiosity, slinks in among the soldiers.

All around Me are false witnesses, uttering lies calculated to increase the anger of the iniquitous judges. They call Me a seducer, a profaner of the Sabbath, a false Prophet, and the servants and menials, stimulated by these accusations, utter cries and execrations against Me.

*　　*

Where, then, were you, O Apostles and Disciples, witnesses of My life and doctrine and of My miracles? Of all those of whom I had every reason to expect help and protection, none was there to defend Me. Abandoned and alone, I faced these ravening wolves!

From all I receive outrages and abuse . . . they strike Me in the face, they spit upon Me, they make of Me a laughing-stock.

And while I offered Myself to be thus ill-used, Peter, whom I had constituted Head of My Church, the same who but a few hours previously had vowed to go with Me to torments and to death—Peter, who might have given testimony of Me, answers a simple question by a flat denial, and follows it by a second one—fear having taken hold of him—he swears that he knows not the man!

Ah, Peter, dost thou deny thy Master? Not only dost thou swear that thou knowest Me not, but at a third question thou utterest horrible imprecations!

*　　*

O My chosen followers, can you fathom the anguish of My Heart?   My own chosen ones deny Me and forsake Me.

As to Peter, I say to you: Have you forgotten the proofs of love you have received from Me and the bonds that unite us?—the reiterated pledges of fidelity till death, of protection from foes, that you made to Me?

If you are weak and timorous, have recourse to Me. Do not trust in your own strength! I alone can sustain you.

Oh, all you who live in the midst of perils . . . be on your guard against danger, for neither had Peter fallen if he had not yielded with temerity to vain curiosity.

And all ye who labour in My vineyard, when the attraction of some merely human enjoyment allures you, fly! But if obedience, zeal for My glory or the good of souls imposes a duty on you, have no fear; I will defend you, and you will pass victoriously through the fire!

While the soldiers led Me to prison, seeing Peter in the crowd, I cast My eyes upon him. . . . Turning, he looked at Me, and forthwith began bitterly to weep for his sin.

It is thus that I look on guilty souls; would that they would look at Me. But do they? If our eyes could but meet. But often I look in vain. . . . I am unnoticed. . . . I call the sinner by name, but receive no answer. . . . I send the trial that might awaken him, and still he slumbers.

Unless your eyes are turned heavenward, you will

in time become as those who are deprived of reason, their faces for ever bent towards earth. Lift up your heads, gaze on your true fatherland, seek your God. You will find that He returns your earnest look, and in His glance are peace and life.

JESUS IN PRISON

Contemplate Me in the prison where I spent the greater part of the night. The soldiers came, and insultingly hustled Me, adding words to injuries.

Tired of their sport, at length they left Me bound and alone in a dark and noisome hole; there, seated on a stone, My aching Body was cramped with the cold.

*   *

COMPARE the prison with the Tabernacle, and especially think of the hearts of those who receive Me.

In the prison I spent only the part of one night, in the Tabernacle, how many nights and days?

In prison I was insulted and ill-treated by enemies; in the Tabernacle most often it is they who call themselves My friends who treat Me thus.

In prison I endured cold and sleeplessness, hunger and thirst, pain and shame, solitude and desertion.

And there passed before My mind's eye all the Tabernacles where in the course of Ages I would lack the shelter of love; the icy-cold hearts that would be as hard and unfeeling as the stones of the prison floor were to My numbed and wounded Body.

How often would I be hungry for souls and thirsty for love? How would I wait in vain for the coming of one I yearned for, hoping and desiring for this slaking of My thirst; how would I be left famishing for generous and faithful hearts? Will they appease this divine craving? Will they come to Me under the pressure of woe and say: "This I offer Thee to console Thy sadness . . . to keep Thee company in Thy solitude." Oh, would that they would so act, with what peace I would inundate their souls. How much fortitude they would win, and how they would gladden My Heart!

While confined in the narrow prison I was abashed and put to shame by the obscene words of those around Me, and My distress was increased by the certainty that the like words would one day fall from lips I love.

When blows and buffets were rained upon Me by the soldiers it recalled to My mind those who would receive Me into hearts fouled by unrepented sin and would shower reiterated blows on Me by their habits of sin (or habitual sins).

And when exhausted and constrained to rise, and unable to help Myself, being bound, they let Me fall to the ground, those who would drag Me to earth by their ingratitude and increase My degradation by turning their backs on Me . . . were present to My tortured mind.

* *

O you who are consecrated to Me, gaze steadfastly upon the Bridegroom of your souls! See Me behind prison bars—think of Me during that night of pain . . . continued, alas, by the anguished loneliness of countless forsaken tabernacles and the coldness of many hearts.

If you are desirous of proving your sympathy, open your heart and let Me find a prison therein.

There bind Me with chains of love.

There clothe Me with assiduous attentions.

Appease My hunger by your generosity.

Assuage My thirst by your zeal.

Comfort Me in My sorrow and abandonment by keeping Me faithful company and wiping out My shame by your purity and uprightness of intention.

And if you desire to be genuine, calm the tumult of your passions that My repose be undisturbed in you.

Then shall My voice resound within you, O Bride of My Heart! And thou shalt never have reason to regret any sacrifice made for love of Me. If tenderly and watchfully thou harbourest Me in the prison of thy heart, I shall be thy reward exceeding great. If thou hast been rest and repose to Me, I shall be the same for thee eternally.

*   *

A CALL TO IMITATE THE DIVINE PRISONER

LISTEN to Me once more, Josefa; these are the wishes of My Heart.

Burning with love at the thought of the many who would follow in My footsteps, I saw them in spirit during those hours in the prison striving to imitate Me closely. I wished them to learn from Me not only to accept suffering and contempt with patience and serenity, but also to extend their love to those who should persecute them.

Like Me, they would rise to the height of offering themselves up in sacrifice for those who ill-treat them.

This prospect enkindled Me with a burning desire to carry out the divine Will in all things. Hence, alone and in much pain, but in close union with the Father, I offered Myself to make amends to His outraged glory.

You, O religious souls, deemed useless and even dangerous in the eyes of the world, on account of the dwelling (prison) you have selected through love, have no fear! In your prison solitude and in momentsof stress, let the world rant against you. Only join your heart yet closer to God, the one object of your affection, and do all you can to repair for the sins and the outrages of men.

MY KINGDOM IS NOT OF THIS WORLD

At dawn next day Caiphas ordered Me to be taken to Pilate, who was to condemn Me to death.

Pilate questioned Me shrewdly, in order to discover a reason for My condemnation, but finding none, his conscience soon told him what a grave injustice he would be guilty of. So in order to evade the responsibility he sent Me to Herod.

Pilate's soul is typical of those tossed between the impulses of grace and the allurement of their own passions, and who, blindly yielding to fears engendered by human respect, i.e. fear of ridicule and excessive self-love, end gradually in setting grace aside.

To all Pilate's questions I answered nothing; but when he said: "Art Thou the King of the Jews?", gravely and with full responsibility I replied: "Thou hast said it. I am a King, but My Kingdom is not of this world."

When an occasion of accepting bravely either humiliation or suffering (even if it could easily be escaped) presents itself, you should answer: "My kingdom is not of this world," that is the reason why I do not seek human favour—I go to my true Fatherland. In the meantime I will generously do my duty, and make no account of the opinion of the world. . . . What is important is not to grow in its esteem, but resisting the enticements of nature, to obey the inspirations of grace. If I am unable to do this alone I will ask for advice, for I know how often self-love and passion blind me and induce me to engage in the paths of evil.

* *

BEFORE HEROD

PILATE therefore commanded Me to be taken before Herod. Now, Herod was an evil-doer, bent only on the satisfaction of his lawless passions by pleasure. He was glad to see Me brought before him, hoping for some entertainment from My words and My miracles.

* *

CONSIDER, O beloved ones, what was the repulsion I felt when brought face to face with so vicious a man, whose reflections and questions, gesticulations and movements filled Me with shame.

O virgin souls, and pure—come, stand by Me and defend Me!

Herod expected replies to his sarcastic remarks, but I opened not My lips, and kept the most profound silence in his presence.

This silence testified to My dignity, for the obscene comments of so perverted a man were not worthy of exchange between him and the All-Pure.

During this interview My Heart was closely united to My Heavenly Father. I desired ardently to shed the last drop of My Blood for souls, and was all inflamed with love at the thought of those who would follow My example and My liberality. Not only did I rejoice during this terrible interrogatory, but I was urged from within to hasten the moment of My ordeal on the Cross.

I therefore allowed Myself to be treated as a fool and arrayed in a white garment, sign of derision, and thus was I led back to Pilate amid the jeers of the multitude.

CONCESSIONS MADE BY PILATE AT THE SCOURGING

Look at Pilate! See that afraid and cowardly man a prey to disturbance; he is at his wit's end, and in order to calm the people's fury he orders Me to be scourged.

Pilate's conduct stands for that of the many whose courage fails them in the face of the demands of the world or of nature, which ought to be met with energy and determination. Instead of obeying conscience and making short work of interior opposition, they yield to one fancy or another, to a slight satisfaction or partial capitulation to passion, and content with not having entirely consented, soothe their consciences with half-measures.

I have but one word for souls of this kind: "Like Pilate, you give Me up to the scourges!" . . . To-day, so much; to-morrow, more. . . . Is it thus that you hope to curb your nature? Before long you will give in all along the line. And if to-day with small provocation, how will you act when temptation is violent, and you have weakened yourself by cowardice in the past?

Contemplate Me, O My Belovèd, being led away as a lamb to the shameful and terrible punishment of the Scourging.

Blow after blow is discharged by the executioners on

My Body, already covered with bruises and broken with fatigue. With whips and knotted cords they strike with such violence that My very bones are shaken and I am torn with innumerable wounds. Bits of My divine Flesh were rent off by the scourges . . . blood flowed from every limb, and I was reduced to such a state of disfigurement as no longer to resemble a human being!

Can you contemplate Me in this sea of sorrow and remain unmoved?

Pity I did not expect from My executioners, but I look for compassion from you, O My chosen people!

See My Wounds! Who has suffered as I have for love of you?

JESUS IS CROWNED WITH THORNS AND DERIDED AS KING

WHEN, exhausted at last by their exertions, these hard and cruel men desisted, they drove deep into My Head a crown of woven thorns, and as they filed before Me they mockingly cried out: "We salute Thee, O King!" And some insulted Me, others savagely struck Me on the Head, and each and all added new agonies to those which already racked My Body.

* *

CONSIDER how by this painful crowning I expiated the sins of pride of those who yield to the tenets of the world and attach excessive importance to its esteem and regard. I allowed the Crowning with Thorns and the exceeding great pain it caused Me that by this humiliation I might specially atone for the pretentious pride of those who depart from the way I have shown them, considering it unworthy of their merit and condition.

No path is contemptible or humbling when it is one marked out by the Will of God. You will seek to delude yourself in vain, if you choose any other or think to do God's Will when you follow your own. Peace and joy can be found only in the accomplishment of God's Will and in entire submission to all He may require of you.

* *

IN this I am especially addressing Myself to those

about to settle their way of life and have too great a regard for their personal inclinations. It may be that they find in her or in him to whom they hope to be united, the prospect of a solidly Christian and devout life, homely virtues and habits of duty, all of which appeal to their affections . . . but should vanity and pride attempt to darken their understanding . . . letting themselves be seized by a craving to have more and better . . . should they renounce their first attraction and look for a companion more in accord with their secret ambitions, how blind and imprudent they would be! No real happiness is to be found in this world. . . . God grant that you may find it in the next, if you persist in exposing it to peril in this life.

*   *

A word to those whom I call to a life of perfection:

How exposed to illusions are those who presumably think themselves to be doing My Will, but who thrust deeply into My Head the Thorns of My Crown.

There are souls whom I covet for My own; knowing them and loving them as I know and love them; I draw them in the direction in which in My Wisdom I have prepared means of attaining sanctity for them. There I will unveil My Heart to them, there they will give Me most love . . . and most souls too.

But what a disappointment when, blinded by secret pride or paltry ambition, and their minds filled with vain thoughts, they end by turning away from the path marked out by love.

O souls that I had picked out, do you think you are doing My Will when you resist the call of grace or refuse through pride to follow Me in the way into which love calls you?

March 23rd, 1923.

BARABBAS PREFERRED TO JESUS

WE shall now continue, Josefa, to make souls understand how through the conceit of pride, many allow themselves to be taken in.

The soldiers therefore brought Me back to Pilate, crowned with thorns and clothed with a purple garment.

Finding no crime in Me worthy of chastisement, Pilate again questioned Me, and asked Me why I did not reply, seeing that he had power to release Me or crucify Me?

To this I answered: "Thou wouldest have no power over Me unless it were given thee from above, but the Scriptures must needs be fulfilled."

After which I resumed My silence, surrendering Myself wholly to God.

Pilate meanwhile, troubled by a message from his wife, and plagued by the remorse of his conscience, and full of fear that the people might turn against him, sought for a pretext to deliver Me. So he presented Me to the people in the pitiable plight to which I had been reduced, offering to release Me and deliver over to them the thief Barabbas; but the multitude cried out with one voice: "Not this man, but Barabbas!"

* *

O all ye who love Me, consider how I was compared

155

to a criminal, degraded beneath the wickedest of men! Hear their cries of rage against Me and their vociferous clamours for My death.

Far from seeking to escape this affront, I lovingly accepted it for you, desirous of showing you that My love was not only leading Me to death, but to the most ignominious of all deaths.

Do not think that I did not feel repugnance and grief in My human nature. . . . I willed to know experimentally all that you would have to undergo, that you might draw strength from My example, and thus fortified, understand how to sacrifice every repugnance when there is question of accomplishing God's Holy Will.

*   *

HERE I once more address Myself to the souls to whom I spoke yesterday. You who are called to perfection, who parley with grace, who shrink from the humiliations of the way I show you, from fear of the strictures of the world, and do all you can to persuade yourselves that you will be more useful in My service, and give Me more glory in some other sphere of life!

To you I make answer: "When I was to be born of poor and humble parents . . . in a stable . . . far from My country and home . . . in the severest season of the year and the coldest of nights . . . did I hesitate, did I refuse?

I then lived for thirty years in the hardest toil in the most obscure of workshops, bearing the contempt and indifference of those for whom my father St. Joseph worked . . . nor did I disdain to help My Mother in the humble and hidden occupations of her poor household. Had I not the necessary skill to exercise the humble trade of carpenter, who at twelve years of age taught the doctors in the Temple? Such was My Father's Will, however, and I could consequently give Him no greater glory.

When I left Nazareth to begin My public life, I could have made Myself known at once as the Messiah and Son of God, so that men should venerate Me and be attentive to My voice. I did not do it, because My one desire was to follow in all things My Father's Will.

And when the hour of My Passion had struck, see how I lovingly embraced that Holy Will; and that, in spite of the cruelty of some, the insults of others, the desertion of My Own, and the ingratitude of the crowds . . . the unspeakable martyrdom of My Body and the intense repugnance of My Soul.

Thus, when you submit yourselves generously to the Will of God in spite of natural repugnance and the opposition of the world—then shall you be closely united to Him and taste ineffable sweetness.

* *

That which I have said to souls that experience this keen repugnance for a humble and hidden life, I repeat to those called on the contrary to spend themselves in the service of the world, when their whole attraction is for a life of solitude and hidden labour.

O Chosen Souls, your happiness and perfection do not lie in following your attraction, nor in living known or unknown to the world, nor in using or hiding the talents you have been endowed with—but consists only and solely in embracing with love God's Will, and

being in perfect conformity with all It requires of you
for His Glory and your perfection.

*   *

ENOUGH for to-day, Josefa; to-morrow we will continue. Love and perform My Will with great alacrity,
since it will mark out the path of Love for you in all
things.

JESUS CONDEMNED TO DEATH

MEDITATE for a moment on the martyrdom of My supremely tender and loving heart at finding Barabbas preferred to Me!

I called to mind the sweet caresses of My Mother when she pressed Me to her heart; the toils of My adopted Father and the care with which he surrounded My life.

I reviewed in spirit the benefits so liberally bestowed by Me on this ungrateful people; how I had given sight to the blind, health to the sick, healing to the lame; how I had fed the multitude in the desert and even raised the dead to life. And see now to what contemptible a state I am reduced, more hated, too, than perhaps any man has ever been; condemned to death as an infamous thief! Pilate has pronounced the sentence. O all ye who love Me, attend and see what are the sufferings of My Heart!

THE DESPAIR OF JUDAS

AFTER the betrayal in the Garden of Olives, Judas wandered away, a fugitive, a prey to the reproaches of his conscience, which taxed him with the most execrable of sacrileges. And when he heard Me condemned to death, he gave himself up to despair and hanged himself.

Who can measure the deep and intense grief of My Heart when I saw this soul so long taught by Love . . . the recipient of My doctrine, one who had so often heard from My lips words of forgiveness for the most heinous crimes, finally throw himself into eternal perdition.

Ah, Judas why not throw yourself at My feet, that I may forgive thee too? If thou art afraid to come near Me because of the raging crowd that surrounds Me, at least glance My way . . . My eyes shall meet thine—even now they are lovingly intent on thee!

O all ye who are immersed in sin and who for a more or less long time have lived as wanderers and fugitives because of your sins . . . if the offences of which you have been guilty have hardened and blinded your hearts, if to grant satisfaction to one or other of your passions you have sunk into evil ways. Ah! when the motives or accomplices of your sin have forsaken yon, and that you realize the state of your soul—O then, do not yield to despair, for as long as a breath of life remains a man may have recourse to Mercy and may ask for pardon.

If you are still young, if the scandals of your life have lowered you in the eyes of the world, do not be afraid. Even if there is reason to contemn you and treat you as a criminal, to insult and cast you off, your God has no wish to see you fall into the flames of Hell. He at least ardently desires to approach you, to forgive you. If you dare not draw near Him, at least let the sighs of your heart reach Him, and at once you will find His kind and fatherly Hand stretched out to lead you to the springs of pardon and of life.

Should it happen that you have spent the greater part of your life in impiety and indifference, and that the sudden proximity of the hour of death fills you with despair and threatens to close your eyes for ever—ah! do not let yourself be taken in. If only one second of life remains to you—make no mistake—there is still time for forgiveness. In that one second you can buy back Eternal Life.

If your whole life has beeen spent in ignorance and error; if you have been a cause of great evil to other men, to Society at large, or to religion; if you have come to realize your state of soul, and your error, do not allow yourself to be crushed by the weight of your sins and of the evil of which you have been the instrument; but with a soul penetrated with deep contrition, throw yourself into an abyss of confidence, and hasten to Him who awaits your return only to pardon you.

*　　*

THE case is the same for the soul that has been faithful

to the observance of My law from childhood, but who has gradually cooled off into a tepid and unspiritual way of living.

Then, maybe, that soul awakens with a shock to realities: life appears to have been a failure, empty, and useless for its salvation and the Evil One attacks it in all sorts of ways and with diabolic envy; he plunges it into discouragement, sadness and dejection . . . magnifies its faults and finally casts it into fear and despair!

O soul who art Mine, give no heed to this ruthless enemy . . . but as soon as My grace touches your heart, before the struggle has even begun, have recourse to Me, beg Me to shed one drop of My Blood over you; come to Me. You know where to find Me under the sacramental veils, lift the veil, and pour out in full trust the story of your wretchedness and falls. Listen reverently to My Words, and have no fears for the past. All has been flooded over in the waves of My love and pity. Your past sins will be only an incentive to humility and will increase your merit; and if you want to give Me the best proof of your love, be wholly convinced of My forgiveness, and that never will your sins equal My Mercy, for it is infinite.

Remain in hiding, Josefa, in the abyss of My love— praying that other souls may be filled with the same sentiments.

THE WAY TO CALVARY

LET us continue, Josefa, and do thou follow Me on the way to Calvary, bowed down under weight of the Cross.

While the loss of the soul of Judas was filling Mine with sadness, the executioners, devoid of every feeling of humanity, now placed a hard and heavy Cross upon My lacerated shoulders. I was to consummate on this Cross the Mystery of Man's Redemption.

Gaze on Me, O Angels of Heaven, slowly toiling towards Calvary. I, the Creator of all earthly marvels, the God to whom all heavenly Spirits pay reverent homage; I carry the holy and blessed wood of the Cross on which I am to breathe forth My last sigh.

O souls who desire faithfully to imitate Me, gaze on Me likewise: I drag Myself wearily forward, My Body broken by many torments, bathed in sweat and blood. I suffer, and there is none to compassionate Me. The crowd, pitiless as ravening wolves, follows in My wake; they fain would devour Me as their prey. So great is My exhaustion and so heavy My Cross, that I fall on the way. . . . See how roughly the inhuman soldiery raise Me to My feet once more . . . one seizes an arm, another tears at My garments that cling to My open sores, a third grasps Me round the neck . . . and again another by the hair. Some shower blows on Me with their clenched fists, and others brutally kick My prostrate Body. The Cross falls upon Me, crushing Me with its weight. My Face is bruised and torn, My Blood mingles with the dust of the highway which blinds My eyes and adheres to the wounds on My Sacred Face. I am become the vilest of creatures, and the most contemptible.

what was going on in order to report it to her. As soon
as the death sentence had been pronounced, she came
forth to meet Me; nor did she leave Me any more till
I had been laid in the tomb.

Same day.

THE MEETING OF JESUS WITH HIS MOTHER

COME yet further with Me; a few steps on you will see
My Blessed Mother, whose heart is pierced with
grief. She comes to meet Me, and that for two reasons:
that, seeing Me, she may have fortitude to endure,
and give Me, her Son, courage to carry on and complete the work of Redemption, helped by the sight of
her heroism.

*   *

CONTEMPLATE the martyrdom of these two hearts.

What does this Mother love more than her Son? See
her powerless to help Him. Moreover, she knows that
the sight of her anguish increases His.

And I? What do I love more than My Mother?
Not only can I offer her no comfort, but I know that
the terrible plight in which she sees Me pierces her
Heart with a sorrow equal to Mine—for if I suffer
death in the Body, she suffers death in her heart.

See those eyes fixed on Mine, as Mine are fixed
on hers! No word is spoken, but what a world of intercourse our two hearts exchange in one heartrending
glance.

*   *

MY Mother was present at all the torments of My
Passion by divine revelation. Some of the disciples,
though afar off for fear of the Jews, tried to find out

165

what was going on in order to report it to her. As soon as the death sentence had been pronounced, she came forth to meet Me; nor did she leave Me any more till I was placed in the tomb.

SIMON OF CYRENE CARRIES THE CROSS
OF JESUS

FOLLOW Me, Josefa, on the Way of the Cross, in the great procession.

Fearing that I might die before Crucifixion, those wicked men looked round for someone to help Me carry the Cross, and for that purpose seized on a man of that neighbourhood called Simon. . . .

Watch him carrying the Cross behind Me, and consider two things: Though he was a man of good will, yet he was mercenary; and if he carried My Cross, it was because he had to yield to force; so, when he began to tire, he allowed the weight to bear more and more on Me, and that is how I twice more fell on the road.

This man helped Me to carry part of My Cross, but not the whole of it.

There are many souls who thus follow in My footsteps, who accept to help Me carry My Cross, but they are troubled about their own rest and consolation. Many consent to come after Me, and that is why they embrace a perfect life, but they do not give up all self-interest, and in many cases allow it to be their *chief* interest. They hesitate, and let My Cross fall when it weighs too heavily. They try to avoid suffering, and are not wholly given to Me; they turn away from humiliation when able, and also from fatigue. They look back regretfully at all they have given up; they try to obtain certain alleviations and conveniences. In a word, they are souls so egoistical and selfish that they follow Me more for their own sakes than for Mine. They will only tolerate what they cannot avoid in the way of suffering, and carry but a small part of My Cross and in such a way as barely to acquire merit indispensable to their salvation. In the next world they will see how far behind they lagged.

On the other hand are a very numerous band of souls who, urged on by the hope of salvation, but still more by the motive of love, are resolute in their determination to follow Me in the way of the Cross. They eagerly embrace the perfect life and devote themselves to My service; they carry not part of the Cross, but the whole of it. Their one desire is to relieve and comfort Me. They offer themselves for that and seek out all that may give Me pleasure. They think neither of reward nor of their own merits, nor of the fatigues and sufferings that may accrue to them, their one object is to show Me their love and console My Heart.

If My Cross comes to them in the shape of illness, if it is hidden under some employment that goes against the grain, or is little adapted to their talents—if it has all the appearance of being the result of forgetfulness on the part of Superiors, or from opposition from those who surround them, they recognize and accept it, whatever it is, with the entire submission of which their will is capable.

Sometimes it happens that, urged by greater love and zeal for souls, they have done what seemed to them best in such or such a circumstance. But things turn out differently from their expectations, and there follows a whole train of humiliations and trials, which fall on them. These souls, solely moved by love, joyfully accept these unexpected consequences of their action; in them they see My Cross—they worship it, offer it up, and use it to procure My greater glory.

These are the souls that truly bear the Cross after Me; their interests and their gain are none other than love; they are repose and glory for My Heart.

Be persuaded that if your self-denial and sufferings appear to bear no fruit, they have not been in vain, they have not been useless; some day you will carry abundant sheaves and reap a great reward.

When a soul loves with all her heart, she does not calculate with suffering and devotedness. Never looking for a reward, she seeks only what she believes to be God's greater glory. She never says "enough" when labour or fatigue are in question . . . and because she loyally acts solely out of love she remains unmoved and untroubled. Still less does she lose her peace of mind; if in certain things she meets with contradiction or persecution, as her actions were prompted only by love, for Love, she leaves results in His Hands.

These are they who are not mercenary—they only want Me to be consoled; they desire only My rest and glory. That, too, is why they have shouldered the whole of My Cross and that they carry its full weight.

March 28th, 1923, Spy-Wednesday.

THE CRUCIFIXION

WE have reached Calvary. The crowd moves uneasily, for the moment is at hand. It is with the utmost difficulty that I still drag Myself along, exhausted with fatigue.

*   *

THREE times I fell on the way to Calvary.

By My first Fall I obtained for sinners rooted in evil, grace for conversion. . . . By My second Fall, encouragement for those weak souls blinded by sadness and anxiety, so that rising up they may make a new beginning in the way of virtue. . . . My third Fall will help souls to rise from sin in the supreme hour of death.

*   *

GLANCE now at the cupidity with which these hardened sinners surround Me . . . some seize hold of the Cross and lay it under Me; the others tear My garments from Me, reopening all My wounds . . . My Blood flows afresh.

*   *

REFLECT for an instant at My shame in seeing Myself thus exposed to the multitude's gaze—what physical pain, what confusion for My soul!

The tunic woven by My Mother, and with which she had so lovingly clothed Me in My Infancy, had grown with My stature—these cruel soldiers despoil

Me of it and draw lots whose it shall be. . . . Think of
the affliction of My Mother, who is a witness of this
terrible scene. How she longs to take possession of the
tunic now impregnated with My Blood.

*   *

THE hour has come! The executioners stretch Me
upon the Cross. They violently extend My arms, that
My hands may reach the holes they have prepared in
the wood. My whole Body is racked with agony . . .
every shock causes My thorn-crowned Head to come
into violent concussion with the Cross . . . now here,
now there, the thorns pierce It on every side, and are
driven deeper and deeper into My Head. Hear the
first sound of the hammer that pierces My right hand
. . . deep into the very earth it resounds. Hark!
they fasten My left hand. The very Heavens tremble,
and the Angels fall prostrate at the sight.

No sound passes My lips—not a murmur escapes
Me.

Having nailed My Hands, they pull pitilessly at My
Feet . . . all My wounds burst open afresh, the nerves
are severed, the bones dislocated. . . . The anguish!
oh, the anguish of it! They pierce My Feet and My
Blood is poured forth on to the ground.

*   *

STAY awhile and contemplate these pierced Hands
and Feet—this body, naked and covered with blood . . .
the Head pierced through and through by cruel thorns,
fouled with mud, bathed in sweat and blood!

Wonder and marvel at My silence, patience and
resignation under such brutal treatment!

Ask thyself, who suffers? Who is the Victim of such

barbarity? JESUS CHRIST, the very Son of God, Maker of Heaven and earth and the sea . . . He who causes the plants to grow and every living thing to prosper . . . He who created man, and whose power sustains all things. . . . Behold Him, fixed in an iron certainty, despoiled of all. But soon what a multitude will follow Me, throwing away fortune, comfort, honour, family and home, and everything the world can give to render Me glory and honour, and the love that is My due.

*   *

BE attentive, O ye Angels of Heaven, and all ye who love Me! The soldiers are about to turn the Cross in order to rivet the nails and thus prevent the weight of My Body from being dragged from the Cross. My Sacred Body gives the kiss of peace to guilty earth . . . and while the air resounds with the sound of hammer on iron, at My Mother's prayer—for she stands impotent to help Me—a witness of My martyrdom;—at her prayer, legions of Angels crowd around to support My Body and prevent it from being grazed by the ground and crushed by the weight of the Cross.

Then the soldiers inhumanly make the air ring with their blows. The earth trembles . . . there is silence in Heaven . . . angelic spirits are prostrate in adoration. . . . A God nailed to the Cross.

*   *

SEE thy Jesus extended on the Cross. He cannot move; exposed, without credit, honour or liberty. Nothing remains to Him.

No one pities Him, none compassionates His sufferings—instead fresh mockeries, more and more pain, is added on to that which He already endures.

If thou lovest Me truly, be ready to resemble Me in everything. Do not refuse to please Me in everything, and spare no efforts to console Me.

*   *

AND now, Josefa, kneel and listen to My words:
  May My Will triumph in thee.
  May My Love consume thee.
  May thy misery glorify Me.

30th March, 1923, Good Friday.

THE SEVEN LAST WORDS

Josefa, thou knowest how I suffer . . . accompany Me to the end and share My sorrows.

The Cross has been raised, the hour of the Redemption of the world has come.

As a public show I am offered up, exposed to the derision of the crowd, yet also to the wonder and love of souls . . . the Cross, hitherto an instrument of torture, on which criminals were made to die, is changed into the light and peace of the world.

Sinners shall draw pardon and life from My Sacred Wounds . . . My Blood shall wash and efface all their filth and foulness.

Pure souls shall come to My Wounds, there to slake their thirst and kindle in their hearts the flames of love . . . there they shall take refuge and for ever make a home.

*   *

FATHER, FORGIVE THEM, FOR THEY KNOW NOT WHAT THEY DO

THEY have not known Him who is their life. On His shoulders they have heaped the fury of their iniquities. But I beseech Thee, Father, heap upon them the full measure of Thy Mercy.

174

TO-DAY THOU SHALT BE WITH ME IN PARADISE

THY Faith in Thy Saviour's Mercy has wiped out all thy offences . . . and it will lead thee to Eternal Blessedness.

WOMAN, BEHOLD THY SON

O MOTHER Mine, behold My Brethren . . . keep them . . . love them. . . . You for whom I died are no longer alone: you have a Mother to whom you can have recourse in every necessity. I have forged between you the closest of unions by giving you My own Mother.

MY GOD, MY GOD, WHY HAST THOU FORSAKEN ME?

. . . YES, henceforth a soul has the right to say to Its God: "Why hast Thou forsaken Me?" After the Mystery of the Redemption was consummated Man became SON OF GOD, Christ is his Brother, eternal Life his heritage.

I THIRST!

O MY Father, I thirst indeed for Thy Glory, and behold . . . now is the hour at hand. Man shall henceforward realize in My Words that Thou indeed hast sent Me, and Thou shalt be glorified.

I thirst for Thy Glory, I thirst for souls, and to appease this thirst I have given the last drop of My Blood. . . .

ALL IS CONSUMMATED!

Now at length the great Mystery of Love, in which a God delivers up to death His own Son, is accomplished.

I came into the world to do Thy Will, O My Father. It is accomplished!

INTO THY HANDS I COMMEND MY SPIRIT

To Thee I give over My Spirit. Thus shall souls that do My Will have the right to say in all truth: "All is consummated . . . My Lord and My God, receive My soul, which I commit into Thy Hands."

* *

JOSEFA, write what thou hast heard. It is My Will that souls should read what thou hast written . . . that the thirsty may thirst no more and the hungry be appeased.

A FEW PRAYERS

ETERNAL Father, Who out of love for souls didst deliver up Thy only Son to the death of the Cross, by His merits and His Heart have pity on the whole world and forgive all the sins committed therein.

Accept the humble reparation of those who love Thee; unite it to the merits of Thy Divine Son, that every act of theirs may be of immense efficacy.

O Eternal Father, have pity on the world; remember that the hour of Justice has not yet struck. It is still the hour of Mercy.

O JESUS, by Thy most loving Heart I beseech Thee to inflame the hearts of all priests and missionaries throughout the world with zeal for Thy Love and Glory. I ask the same grace for those who preach Thy Word, that burning with holy zeal they may snatch souls from the Evil One and lead them all to the harbour of Thy divine Heart, there to glorify Thee for ever and ever. Amen.

CPSIA information can be obtained
at www.ICGtesting.com
Printed in the USA
LVHW090048090223
738971LV00008B/119